Angelomorphic Christology and the Exegesis of Psalm 8:5 in Tertullian's Adversus Praxean

An Examination of Tertullian's Reluctance to Attribute Angelic Properties to the Son of God

Edgar G. Foster

UNIVERSITY PRESS OF AMERICA,® INC.
Lanham • Boulder • New York • Toronto • Oxford

Copyright © 2005 by
University Press of America,® Inc.
4501 Forbes Boulevard
Suite 200
Lanham, Maryland 20706
UPA Acquisitions Department (301) 459-3366

PO Box 317
Oxford
OX2 9RU, UK

All rights reserved
Printed in the United States of America
British Library Cataloging in Publication Information Available

Library of Congress Control Number: 2005930059
ISBN 0-7618-3313-7 (clothbound : alk. ppr.)
ISBN 0-7618-3314-5 (paperback : alk. ppr.)
ISBN 978-0-7618-3314-7

∞™ The paper used in this publication meets the minimum
requirements of American National Standard for Information
Sciences—Permanence of Paper for Printed Library Materials,
ANSI Z39.48—1992

Contents

Vita Tertulliani in Breve	v
Preface	xiii
Acknowledgements	xv
Introduction	xvii
List of Abbreviations	xxiii

1 Daniélou and the Angelomorphic Christology of Tertullian — 1
  A. Recent Christological Studies Concerning Angelomorphism — 1
  B. The Question of Angelomorphic Christology in
     Tertullian's Writings — 3
  C. Problemata Associated with Daniélou's Historical Method — 4
  D. The Ontological Chasm and Tertullian's
     Angelomorphic Aversion — 9
  E. Critiquing Daniélou's Analysis of Adversus Praxean 3 — 9

2 The Exegesis of Psalm 8:5 in the Pre-Nicenes — 19
  A. Overview of Gnosticism — 19
  B. Valentinian Ontology and Christology — 20
  C. The Orthodox Response to Gnosticism — 21
  D. Exegesis of Ps 8:5 by the Greek and Latin Pre-Nicenes — 26
  E. Tertullian's Exegetical Approach to Ps 8:5 — 29

3 Formal Introduction to Adversus Praxean — 41
  A. The Identity of Praxeas — 41
  B. Tertullian's Opposition to Praxean Christology — 42

Contents

	C. Tertullian's Extended Case against Praxeas	44
	D. The Praxean Attempt to Expel Prophecy from Rome	45
	Findings	47
4	The Distinction between the Sermo Dei and Son qua Son	53
	A. Ratio	53
	B. Sermo	54
	C. Sophia	55
	D. Distinguishing the Eternal Ratio from the Temporal Filius	55
	Findings	59
5	Tertullian's Exegesis of Ps 8:5 in Adversus Praxean	63
	A. The Preexistent Son and Adversus Praxean 9	63
	B. Adversus Praxean 16	68
	C. Adversus Praxean 23	70
	D. Kearsley and Tertullian's Interpretation of Ps 8:5 in Adv Prax 9	71
	E. Critique of Kearsley's Treatment	72

Conclusion — 79
   Implications of This Study — 80

Appendix — 83
   I. Persona and Tertullian — 83
   II. Substantia and Tertullian — 84
   III. Sophia and Angelomorphic Christology in Adversus Praxean — 85
   IV. Stoicism and Substance — 86
   V. Carthage and Christianity — 87
   VI. Tertullian and the Regula Fidei — 87
   VIII. Omnipotence of Christ in Tertullian — 89

Bibliography — 93

Index — 99

Biographical Sketch of Author — 101

Vita Tertulliani in Breve

Quintus Septimius Florens Tertullianus (Tertullian) was born ca. 160 CE and died ca. 220 CE.[1] The noted church apologist dwelled in Carthage (North Africa),[2] a province of Rome.[3] Indeed, it was in Carthage that Tertullian received a first-rate education[4], which may have made it possible for him to become a jurist[5] before his conversion to Christianity between the years 193–197 CE. Upon becoming a Christian, Tertullian subsequently produced approximately thirty significant theological documents that scholars classify as apologetic, dogmatico-polemic or practico-ascetic.[6]

Adversus Praxean is manifestly a controversial treatise (*liber controversiae*) that Tertullian wrote ca. 213 CE to counter a perceived heretical notion set forth by an enigmatic individual named Praxeas.[7] It is therefore no wonder that this document noticeably functions as a sublime example of Tertullian's "burning eloquence, biting satire, and forcible logic."[8] This polemical work directed at an ancient influential non-orthodox church figure contains 31 sections (*capita*) that Tertullian appears to have structured in a manner analogous to classical rhetorical speeches composed by either Marcus Fabius Quintilian (35–95 CE) or Marcus Tullius Cicero (106–43 BCE). *Adversus Praxean* thus stands as a clear testimony to Tertullian's stylistic adroitness and rhetorical expertise.

Adversus Praxean commences with a standard literary introduction (*exordium*),[9] a customary delineation of preliminary facts (*narratio*)[10] and then proceeds to Tertullian's skillful advancement of his rhetorical case by means of incisive logical arguments (*confirmatio*) that appear to support the charges he forcefully brings against the adversary, Praxeas.[11] Tertullian next proffers a variety of counterarguments (*reprehensio*) in order to subvert the theological position of his opponent before he employs the familiar rhetorical device *pathos* (i.e. an appeal to the emotions of one's audience).[12] Ulteriorly, the apologist from Carthage concludes his argument with a dynamic literary expansion or *amplificatio*. The fruits of *Adversus Praxean* are accordingly apparent and decisive: "Tertullian knew how a rhetorician convinces his hearers, wins them over to himself and incites them against others."[13] The ancient Carthaginian carefully studied his forebears, astutely emulating and innovating their elocutionary styles. Hardly any writer of antiquity possessed Tertullian's ability to manipulate the Latin language in such a vibrant or persuasive manner.[14]

After noting the similarities between Tertullian's declamatory methods and those utilized by other noted rhetoricians of antiquity, Sider concludes that Tertullian seems to implement familiar literary devices with acute flexibility.[15] In other words, he is not beholden to the proven techniques of his predecessors, but shows his creative or innovative side when using the tools of classical rhetoric. Unsurprisingly, one church historian consequently remarks that it is impossible to suffer *ennui* while perusing the vivid contents of Tertullian's literary corpus.[16] He readily avails himself of rhetorical procedures that unfailingly sustain the interest of his readers. Especially is this tendency evident in *Adversus Praxean*, where Tertullian overtly displays his entire arsenal of wit, scriptural proof-texts and rhetorical devices in order to dispose of the heretical teachings of his opponent. Tertullian also vigorously endeavors to demonstrate that the Father, Son and Holy Spirit are not three self-identical divine modes of being but distinct deific *personae*.[17] The skilled *rhetor*, however, highlights the putative uniqueness of each divine *persona* by characterizing the Father as the whole divine substance (*pater enim tota substantia est*) in contrast to the Son or Spirit of God whom he depicts as respective portions of the one divine substance (*portiones totius*).[18] It thus seems that Tertullian's so-called Trinitarian theology posits a subordination of essence with respect to the Son and Holy Spirit.

Nevertheless, Bethune-Baker maintains that such "crudities of thought" do not detract from Tertullian's overall treatment of the three purported deific persons (*tres personae*) constituting the Godhead.[19] Bethune-Baker, along with other historians of Christian dogma and thought, considers the pistic[20] defense that *Adversus Praxean* contains to be prototypical from a doctrinal standpoint and peerless vis-à-vis its stylistic aspects. It is little wonder that Jürgen Moltmann observes: "The Fathers learnt from Tertullian, even if they did not mention his name. He perceived the problems more clearly than anyone before him, and the brilliance of his language and his skill in definition made new answers possible."[21] Though he therefore writes (from time to time) in an admittedly macabre fashion,[22] Tertullian undeniably shaped Latin theology for all time.[23] He was an apologist *par excellence*.

In view of the foregoing data, we should not be surprised to hear modern historians hailing Tertullian as "The most penetrating exegete of the whole ancient church."[24] Others call him: "The greatest of the early Latin writers."[25] Unfortunately, certain Christian scholars are motivated to brand some of the material found in the ardent African's so-called Montanist writings as "heretical" since they think Montanism (a movement which Tertullian evidently joined) was a form of Christianity that the church eventually deemed heretical.[26] While Tertullian may have converted to Montanism, however, there seems to be little evidence that he ever succumbed to heresy *per se*. Cyprian of Carthage who considered Tertullian "the master" may very well establish this point (*De Viris Illustribus* 53). On the other hand, Jerome appears to[27] praise Tertullian's genius while condemning his "heresy." He is nevertheless very sympathetic with respect to Tertullian's supposed deviation from the historic Christian faith.[28]

We do not know the exact year that Tertullian possibly became a Montanist, but it appears that he may have embraced the New Prophecy (*nova prophetia*) no later than 207 CE.[29] His theological treatises seem to show pronounced signs of the ecstatic group's influence after this period. In fact, *Adversus Praxean* is one ostensible Montanist document that theologians commonly differentiate from the more "catholic" treatises of Tertullian.[30] As stated earlier, the apologist's association with the New Prophecy occasionally has resulted in certain Christian historians minimizing the apologetic efforts of one who accomplished so much for historic orthodoxy during his lifetime. Yet, regardless of his personal "demise" in later years, Tertullian's contribution to the church is indisputable:

> When, with an imagination that is vivid enough to reproduce the situation, the circumstances, and the temperament of the man, and a judgement that is based upon a calm review of his theology in its historical setting, we draw near to Tertullian, we shall recognize in him, despite his failings and limitations, one of the noblest characters and greatest thinkers of the Christian Church.[31]

While there are a number of prominent figures one could focus on when investigating the Christological outlook of the early Latin Church, the major luminary in this movement is Tertullian. He is the preeminent *dramatis persona* in early Latin Christianity. This ancient North African skillfully shaped western theology in a lasting and unforgettable way.

NOTES

1. Evans suggests that Tertullian died in 240 CE, based on a passage in Jerome that indicates the apologist lived to an advanced age (*ad decrepitam aetatem*). See

E. Evans, *Adversus Praxean* (London: SPCK, 1948), 2. However, Bardenhewer thinks Tertullian fell asleep in death ca. 220 CE. Cf. O. Bardenhewer, *Patrology: The Lives and Works of the Fathers of the Church*, trans. Thomas J. Shahan (St. Louis: B. Herder, 1908), 179.

2. Modern Tunisia.

3. *Vide* appendix V of the present work.

4. Christine Trevett cites Jerome's dictum (*Ep*. 70.5), "Quid Tertulliano eruditius, quid acutius" when relating Tertullian's well-known facility with rhetoric, Latin, and Greek. See *Montanism: Gender, Authority, and the New Prophecy* (Cambridge: Cambridge University Press, 1996), 68.

5. At one time, Tertullian's legal background was a historical given. Historians have since called his juristic career into question and now fervently debate the issue. While the "dust" from Timothy Barnes' challenge vis-à-vis Tertullian's legal training has not yet subsided, Roy Kearsley points out that the "apologist's thought" moves and breathes in the "atmosphere of law," *Tertullian's Theology of Divine Power* (Carlisle and Cumbria: Rutherford House by Paternoster Press, 1998), 12. Gerald Bray takes issue with the thesis advanced by Kearsley, however. He thinks there is hardly any historical indication that Tertullian was a professional jurist. Consult *Holiness and the Will of God: Perspectives on the Theology of Tertullian* (Atlanta: John Knox Press, 1979), 33–34. The question is by no means settled, but Kearsley's observation regarding Tertullian's thought seems to be a perspicacious one.

6. Bardenhewer, *Patrology*, 179–180. Evans classifies Tertullian's literary works as apologetic, controversial and disciplinary treatises. See Evans, *Adversus Praxean*, 3. Johannes Quasten's classifications mirror those of Evans. Cf. Quasten, *Patrology*, 3 vol. (Utrecht: Spectrum, 1962–1964), 255–317.

7. Aloys Grillmeier, *Christ in Christian Tradition: From the Apostolic Age to Chalcedon* (451), trans. J. S. Bowden (London: Mowbray, 1965), 141. See also W. H. C. Frend, *The Rise of Christianity* (Philadelphia: Fortress Press, 1984), 345.

8. Bardenhewer, *Patrology*, 180.

9. See *Adv Prax* 1.

10. Sider points out that the *narratio* provides an account of the events that function as the *raison d'être* of the rhetorical treatise. The *narratio* also indicates "the speaker's intended manner of treatment." That is, it sets forth the primary areas of dispute, though Sider does add that some students of rhetoric attribute this function to the *propositio* or *partitio*. See Robert D. Sider, *Ancient Rhetoric and the Art of Tertullian* (London: Oxford University Press, 1971), 21. Quintilian notes that "most authorities" (plurimis auctoribus) think forensic speeches have five parts, namely, the *exordium*, the *narratio*, *confirmatio*, *refutatio*, and the *peroratio* (*Institutio Oratoria* 3.9.1–9).

11. Cf. *Adv Prax* 2.

12. Aristotle, *Rhet* 1418a.

13. Hans von Campenhausen, *The Fathers of the Church* (Peabody: Hendrickson, 1998), 10.

14. Ibid., 8–9.

15. Sider, *Ancient Rhetoric*, 21–24. For a classical discussion of the need for flexibility in formulating speeches, see Quintilian's *Institutio Oratoria* 2.13.5–8.

16. Campenhausen, *Fathers*, 9.

17. *Adv Prax* 2.

18. Ibid. 9. Sydney Mellone echoes the sentiments of Tertullian, writing: "The Father is wholly essential Being (*substantia*): the Son is derived from the Whole as a part thereof (*portio totius*)," in *Leaders of Early Christian Thought* (Lindsey P, 1954), 178. Nevertheless, Mellone cites Souter who thinks that though Tertullian does not affirm the eternal generation doctrine and regards the Son as but a *portio totius*, the Son is still God (according to Tertullian) since "He came from the essence of God Himself, thus being from the essence of the Whole and part of the Whole," Ibid. But this notion is problematic for a number of reasons. If the Λογος, based on Tertullian's formulation, possesses the entire complex of divine properties and is fully God (*vere deus*), then why is He not an eternal divine *personae*? What is more, Mellone elsewhere writes that Tertullian believes that the Son is subordinated vis-à-vis his essence and not just per function. How can this be the case if the Son is "the essence of the Whole"?

19. James Franklin Bethune-Baker, *An Introduction to the Early History of Christian Doctrine to the Time of the Council of Chalcedon* (London: Methuen, 1919), 144.

20. Following the work of Nicolai Hartmann and Abraham Kuyper, Herman Dooyeweerd posits at least fifteen irreducible modal aspects (spheres of being), which include the pistic sphere, see *A New Critique of Theoretical Thought,* trans. David H. Freeman and William S. Young, 4 vol. (Ontario, Paideia Press, 1984), 2:298. Dooyeweerd defines πίστις as "the terminal function of human existence in the transcendental direction of time," ibid. Πίστις is thus a universal phenomenon that is not restricted to Christian believers. Moreover, the pistic region of being is transcendental and is in this way an "irreducible function in the whole process of knowledge" (Ibid., 2:299). Yet, the pistic sphere, as seen in the case of Tertullian and other early Christian apologists, can acquire a soteriological significance when one directs πίστις toward the God who sent Christ and raised Him from the dead. One can also view Christ as the object of πίστις since the Son of God explains the Father to humankind (Jn 1:18; 14:1).

21. Jurgen Moltmann, *The Trinity and the Kingdom: The Doctrine of God*, trans. Margaret Kohl (New York: Harper and Row, 1981), 137. Although historians of dogma generally consider *Adversus Praxean* to be "a remarkable foreshadowing" of the Council of Nicea, Bardenhewer notes that Tertullian: "does not avoid a certain subordinationism," *Patrology*, 185. Louis Berkhof similarly thinks that Tertullian's treatment of the Trinity doctrine involves "an unwarranted subordination of the Son to the Father." See Berkhof's *Systematic Theology* (London: Banner of Truth, 1971), 82. Moltmann also points to problematic aspects of Tertullian's Trinitarian formulation. He notes that while Tertullian raised Christian theological discourse to a new level, he also produced more questions. See *Trinity and the Kingdom*, 137. Pelikan observes possible traces of binitarian thinking in Tertullian and other early church fathers in *The Christian Tradition: A History of the Development of Doctrine*, 5 vol. (Chicago and London: University of Chicago Press, 1971), 1:197. For further information, consult Tertullian's *De Orat* 1.1–2.

22. Tertullian seems to take a little too much delight in describing God's eschatological judgment: "How vast a spectacle then bursts upon the eye! What there excites

my admiration? What my derision? Which sight gives me joy? Which rouses me to exultation? As I see so many illustrious monarchs, whose reception into the heavens was publicly announced, groaning now in the lowest darkness with great Jove himself, and those, too, who bore witness of their exultation; governors of provinces, too, who persecuted the Christian name, in fires more fierce than those with which in the days of their pride they raged against the followers of Christ" (*De Spec* 30).

23. Campenhausen, *Fathers*, 5. Certain historians (e.g. Daniélou) would contest Campenhausen's claim. To the contrary, these scholars would place Minucius Felix at the beginning of the Latin Church. The position taken in this work is that Tertullian is the first noted theological personality in the West: he initially and essentially shaped Western Christianity. James Morgan fittingly observes: "In doctrine and language he is the great pioneer of Western Christianity," see *The Importance of Tertullian in the Development of Christian Dogma* (London: Kegan Paul, Trench, Trubner, 1928), ix.

Quasten, though thinking that certain historical accounts regarding Tertullian are legendary in character, nevertheless concedes: "Except for St. Augustine, Tertullian is the most important and original ecclesiastical author in Latin," *Patrology*, 247.

24. Campenhausen, *Fathers*, 5.

25. Edmund Fortman, *The Triune God: A Historical Study of the Doctrine of the Trinity* (Eugene: Wipf and Stock, 1999), 107. Gerald O'Collins further writes that Tertullian pioneered the Latin "trinitarian vocabulary," in *Christology: A Biblical, Historical, and Systematic Study of Jesus Christ* (Oxford: Oxford University Press, 1995), 182. This claim is not necessarily invalid, but it seems more accurate to say that the church appropriated the Latin Trinitarian vocabulary that Tertullian employed, though he himself did not apply the term *trinitas* to the Christian deity per se (Morgan, *The Importance of Tertullian*, 103). Tertullian's language with respect to the *trinitas* apparently refers to the divine economy (God's historical arrangement for reconciling humanity to Himself through Christ Jesus) and evidently does not really begin to concer itself with the inner constitution of the Godhead. While Morgan concludes that Cyprian was the first pre-Nicene to use the term *trinitas* as a "name of the Deity" in *On the Lord's Prayer*, it appears that not even Cyprian employs the word in this fashion. See *On the Lord's Prayer* 7.22. Cyprian may, however, come close to attributing the nominal *trinitas* to God in *Ep.* 72 during his exposition of Mt 28:19–20.

26. Scott Butler, Norman Dahlgren and David Hess, *Jesus, Peter and the Keys* (Santa Barbara: Queenship Publishing, 1996), 216–217.

27.

28. See Christine Mohrmann, *Vigiliae Christianae* 5 (1951), pp. 111–112. Frend makes a persuasive case for Tertullian becoming a Montanist. See *The Rise of Christianity*, 349–350, 364.

29. C. Trevett thinks that Tertullian became a Montanist no later than 207. His sentiments, however, could have predated this time. Trevett also notes that Tertullian called Montanism, the *nova prophetia*, but the Montanists no doubt used the expression self-referentially as well. See Trevett, *Montanism*, 71. David Aune concurs with this assessment in *Prophecy in Early Christianity and the Ancient Mediterranean World* (Grand Rapids: Eerdmans, 1983), 313. Tertullian also endowed Montanism with "an impact on the writing of church history which otherwise it would not have

had," Trevett, *Montanism*, 67. The opponents of the *nova prophetia* also gave them the designation, Cataphrygians. Only later did the ecstatic movement come to be known as the Montanists. Consult Ronald E. Heine, *The Montanist Oracles and Testimonia* (Patristic Monograph Series 14. Macon: Mercer University Press, 1989), x.

30. Tertullian's allusions to the Paraclete in *Adversus Preaxean* may well have reference to Montanus, who evidently thought of himself as an inspired instrument of God, though Pelikan appears to think it is very difficult to substantiate this position from the references to the Paraclete in *Adversus Praxean*.

31. Robert Edwin Roberts, *The Theology of Tertullian* (London: Epworth, 1924), 252. Timothy Barnes writes: "Tertullian's later writings receive abuse and condemnation in subsequent ages. Many of the charges are unmerited." See *Tertullian: A Historical and Literary Study* (Oxford: Clarendon Press, 1985), 83. He concludes that Tertullian was bold enough to sound forth an "unpalatable truth," namely, that "the church is not a conclave of bishops" but functions as the locus of the Holy Spirit. In other words, where the Spirit of God is, there is the church. See *De Pudi* 21.17: "ecclesia spiritus per spiritalem hominem, non ecclesia numerus episcoporum."

William Tabbernee believes it is "highly unlikely" that Tertullian "ever separated from the catholic church at all" and he avers that he surely did not found the group known as the Tertullianists, which was a post-Montanist sect. He documents these points in *Montanist Inscriptions and Testimonia: Epigraphic Sources Illustrating the History of Montanism* (Macon: Mercer University Press, 1997), 475–476. While Pope Gelasius supposedly condemned Tertullian's works in the *Decretum Gelasianum*, patristic scholars note that this document could well be the result of a forgery. For a penetrating critique of Barnes' overall historical project, however, see W. H. C. Frend's article in the *Classical Review* 24 (1974) pp. 72–76.

Preface

Angelomorphic Christology is a useful descriptive tool that one can employ to elucidate the doctrine of Christ set forth in the NT. While it is somewhat anachronistic to speak of any "doctrine" appearing in the Greek Scriptures of Christianity, the language of systematic theology with its talk of various doctrines does provide a way to structure the NT account of Christ Jesus. We will therefore use such theological language in this study.

For historical reasons, we will initiate this investigation with the personal story of Tertullian. R. G. Collingwood is renowned for thinking of history in terms of a re-telling of factical (i.e. historical) narratives. The story we are about to "re-tell" here represents one of many accounts related by ecclesiastical historians; it does not claim to be the last word on the subject. In fact, after this inquiry, we are convinced that many aspects of Tertullian's project will remain enshrouded in mystery. The modest goal of this study, therefore, is to provide a different and alternative perspective on Tertullian of Carthage, in particular, to outline a different perspective with respect to his doctrine of Christ.

At this point, a word must also be said about the sources used in this study. The numbering system for *Adversus Praxean* that I have used follows the scheme of E. Evans. When citing *De Anima*, we adhere to J. Waszink's numbering; For Tatian's *Oratio*, I employ Whittaker's text. The works of E. Evans, J. Waszink, J. Pelikan, J. Daniélou, A. Blaise, W. H. C. Frend, F. E. Peters, C. Gieschen, P. Carrell, E. Fortman, M. Alfs, R. Kearsley, and J. Morgan all served as indispensable works during the research portion of this work as did Tertullian.org. It has been a didactic experience interacting with the scholars mentioned hitherto. This monograph would not have been possible without the previously mentioned resources.

Edgar Foster
Lenoir, N.C.
November 20, 2003

Acknowledgements

I wish to thank all those who have supported me or provided helpful critiques of my work. Philip Blosser, Heinz Schmitz, Donald Jacobs, Ralph Patrick, Marjorie Monroe, John Blakey, Daniel Beckert and my wife Sylvia were vital in helping me get through the writing process. Ian Hazlett was also a very helpful supervisor. I would never have been able to complete this work without his input and support. I am also thankful to the Rotary Foundation for funding my research in Glasgow and showing me immense hospitality while I stayed there. Lastly, I would like to dedicate this work to my parents, Ed and Eleanor Foster. They have sustained me for years and continue to do so. *Probare autem tam aperte debebis ex scripturis* (*Adv Prax* 11).

Introduction

This study will seek to answer three questions related to Tertullian's doctrine of Christ. The three queries we will explore herein are: (1) Did Tertullian eradicate every vestige of angelomorphism from his doctrine of Christ? (2) Does he think there is a gaping ontological abyss that markedly separates Christ and the holy angels? (3) Why was Tertullian reluctant to identify the Son of God as an angel?

In addressing question (1), this study will demonstrate that Jean Daniélou seems to employ the terminology "Angelomorphic Christology" where other scholars use the terminology "Angelic Christology." This investigation argues that he may thereby be culpable of semiotic imprecision or catachresis. The reason we deem this point significant is that Daniélou contends Tertullian categorically rejected all forms of Angelomorphic Christology. The results that derive from the present investigation, however, indicate otherwise. We will therefore initiate this analysis of Tertullian's body of writings with a critique of Daniélou's work regarding Latin Christianity.

Regarding query (2), it seems Daniélou further maintains that Tertullian is averse to identifying Christ as an angel since the Latin apologist allegedly believes that there is a radical distinction between Christ and the holy angels of God. Nevertheless, while Daniélou imputes this view to Tertullian, we will contend that Tertullian's use of *monarchia* allows us to fuse the ontological divide that purportedly separates Christ and the angels *per essentiam*. We will also examine this issue in chapter one.

In order to answer question (3), we will document the diverse exegetical approaches that Tertullian and other pre-Nicenes employ with respect to the "minoration"[1] saying at Ps 8:5: "You have made him a little lower than the heavenly beings [i.e. angels]" (NIV). It is noteworthy that Tertullian only applies this Bible verse to the Messiah, Jesus Christ. In particular, he refers the verse in Psalms to the pre-angelophanic and pre-incarnate Son as well as to the enfleshed Logos. Chapters two and five will elucidate these claims and they will provide evidence that demonstrates Tertullian believed the pre-existent Son of God was made inferior to the angels when His Father temporally generated Him

A. DELINEATION OF TERMS EMPLOYED IN THIS STUDY

Mentally grasping the nomenclature of Angelomorphic Christology is vital since a number of contemporary studies that explore the doctrine of Christ articulate His exemplary personhood and work in terms of angelic or Angelomorphic Christology.[2] We have not found any recent study, however, that extensively deals with the presence or absence of Angelomorphic themes in the writings of Tertullian. Most works only provide a summary treatment of Tertullian's Angelomorphic Christology or lack thereof, briefly citing one or two references in passing.[3] Therefore, this inquiry should contribute to future investigations of Christ's relationship with the holy angels of God in a meaningful way.

Throughout this study, we will be working with terms such as Angelomorphic Christology, angelic Christology, angelophanic Christology and angelomorphism. It is necessary to define these terms at the outset in order to avoid confusion later. Below, we will distinguish between the four referring expressions that this study will utilize.

Biblical scholars and theologians generally avail themselves of four kinds of terminology to delineate the ways in which they believe Christ is related to the holy angels:

(1) Angel or angelic Christology is the theological concept that Martin Werner infamously maintained the early Christian congregation espoused. In Werner's estimation, the doctrine that teaches the Son is a creaturely spiritual essence produced in the same or similar fashion as other holy created spirit beings was a primordial Christian theological paradigm:

> What has provided historians of doctrine for more than a century with an occasion for discussion has been the fact that Justin could conceive in one category the Logos-Son together with the "host of the other good angels, of like being to him," and that he set this angel-host, together with the Logos-Christ, before the (prophetic) Spirit.[4]

Naturally, historians of dogma generally have not embraced Werner's reconstruction of the primitive or pre-Nicene doctrine of Christ's person and work.

In fact, they have adamantly resisted his suggestion that angel Christology was the most ancient ecclesiastical formulation of the Son's person and work. Chapter one will accordingly discuss Werner's contribution to the study of Christ as an angel qua angel (whether in form or essence). It will then review recent assessments of his work.

(2) Angelomorphic Christology refers to the doctrine or complex of doctrines that contend Christ now and again assumes the form or external appearance of an angel during OT and NT angelophanies but is not necessarily an angel according to His nature (i.e. substance). Stuckenbruck notes that Christ is sometimes "made to appear among a series of angels."[5] At other times, He evidently manifests Himself "as one who incorporates features frequently attributed to angels." The theological doctrine, "Angelomorphic Christology" aptly describes such manifestations, argues Stuckenbruck.[6] This particular type of Christology is clearly phenomenologically oriented.[7] It attempts to provide a descriptive account of the Son's appearances in angelic settings (Rev 14:6–20) without pronouncing judgment on His seeming divine *ontos*.

(3) Stuckenbruck prefers to employ the referring expression "angelophanic Christology" or Angelomorphic Christology over against using the terminology "angelic Christology."[8] Both Christopher Rowland and Stuckenbruck advocate this terminological usage since they argue that Christ is only an angel ostensibly in certain OT or NT angelophanies. He is not, they seem to aver, really a created supernatural spirit being, but the fully divine Son of God.[9]

Stuckenbruck limits the term "Angelomorphic Christology" to occasions when Christ either reveals Himself among a series of angels or provisionally incorporates the attributes of created heavenly beings without becoming an angel ontologically.[10] He further avails himself of the expression "angel Christology" in order to speak of moments when the Scriptures identify Christ as an angel (*ex officio*) or possibly highlight His provisional angelic "nature." Moreover, Stuckenbruck appears to use "Angelomorphic" or "Angelophanic" somewhat synonymously (while preserving the respective shades of meaning for each adjective) as we will do throughout the course of this study.[11] The difference between the two adnominals is that the former descriptive term emphasizes the form assumed or manifested by Christ while the latter adjectival expression stresses the act of manifestation or appearance simply and solely.

(4) A broader category that aptly describes what is often found in the documents of ancient and Second Temple Judaism as well as early Christian works is angelomorphism *simpliciter*. Angelomorphism refers to the phenomenon wherein exalted divine figures assume angelic or semi-divine forms. Such manifestations are not limited to the angelophanies of God's Son.

Judaism speaks of such exalted figures as Adam, Abel, Enoch, Gabriel, Michael and Metatron.[12]

B. THE GOAL OF THIS STUDY

This study will suggest that it is the Son as such, whom the Father makes inferior to the angels. That is, God causes the pre-existent Son to become less than the angels for a time. In order to be *au fait* with the main argument that we will essay in the following pages, the reader will need to make a formal distinction between the Word of God and the Son *qua* Son. This particular aspect of Tertullian's Christology is somewhat exigent or formidable. Chapter four will attempt to sort out the Christological titles that Tertullian uses to formulate his doctrine of Christ and clearly show the formal distinction between the Word of God and the Son.

Subsequent to the examination of *Adversus Praxean*, we will submit that while Tertullian is reluctant to call the Son an angel, it is not because he thinks there is a radical ontological differentiation between the Son *qua* Son and God's holy angels. To the contrary, Tertullian believes that God made the pre-existent, pre-incarnate and pre-angelophanic Son as such lower than the angels when He generated Christ from His own substance. This divine paternal emanative act that results in the Word's "lessening" implies that the ontological divide suggested by Daniélou may not be that extensive after all. We will now analyze Daniélou's analysis of Tertullian's view toward Angelomorphic Christology.

NOTES

1. The term "minoration" refers to the subordinate position of Christ. In particular, this study uses the term to delineate the result of the Father making the Son less than the angels. The Son becomes inferior to the angels by virtue of the Father's lowering him in status and possibly being.

2. Some studies include: L.A. Brighton. "*The Angel of Revelation: An Angel of God and an Icon of Jesus Christ*" (Ph.D. Diss. St Louis University, 1991); Robert Gundry. "Angelomorphic Christology in the Book of Revelation," *SBL Seminar Papers* 33 (1994) 662–78; Loren T. Stuckenbruck, *Angel Veneration and Christology: A Study in Early Judaism and in the Christology of the Apocalypse of John* (Tübingen, J. C. B. Mohr, 1995). We might add that Stuckenbruck prefers to speak of "angelophanic" as opposed to "angelomorphic Christology" (Ibid. 209ff). This study will consistently refer to Angelomorphic Christology, although we will use the terminology "angelophanic Christology" intermittently and somewhat interchangably.

3. Even the comprehensive work by Charles Gieschen only provides a brief treatment of Tertullian's work. See *Angelomorphic Christology: Antecedents and Early Evidence* (Leiden: Brill, 1998), 193–94.

4. *The Formation of Christian Dogma: An Historical Study of Its Problem*, trans. S. G. F. Brandon (London: Black, 1957), 135. See Justin's 1 *Apology* 6.1–2.

5. Stuckenbruck, *Angel Veneration*, 208.

6. Ibid.

7. Darrell D. Hannah, *Michael and Christ: Michael Traditions and Angel Christology in Early Christianity* (Tübingen: Mohr Siebeck, 1999), 13.

8. Stuckenbruck, *Angel Veneration*, 209.

9. Ibid.

10. Ibid. 208.

11. Ibid.

12. See Darrell L. Bock, *Blasphemy and Exaltation in Judaism: The Charge against Jesus in Mark 14:53-65* (Grand Rapids: Baker, 2000), 115–179.

List of Abbreviations

Adv Haer	Against Heresies (Irenaeus)
Adv Herm	Against Hermogenes (Tertullian)
Adv Marc	Against Marcion
Adv Prax	Against Praxeas
Adv Val	Against the Valentinians
Apol	Apology
Contra Celsum	Against Celsus (Origen)
Contra Noet	Against Noetus (Hippolytus)
Cor	Corinthians
De Anima	Concerning the Soul (Tertullian)
De Carne	On the Flesh of Christ
De Exhortatione	Exhortation to Chastity
De Orat	On Prayer
De Paen	On Penitence
De Prae Haer	On the Prescription for Heretics
De Prin	On First Principles (Origen)
De Pud	On Modesty (Tertullian)
De Res	Concerning the Resurrection of the Flesh
De Spec	The Shows
De Virg	On the Veiling of Virgins
Ep	Epistles (Jerome)
Institutes	Divine Institutes (Lactantius)
JBL	Journal of Biblical Literature
Jn	Gospel of John
JTS	Journal of Theological Studies
LSJ	Liddell-Scott Greek-English Lexicon

LXX	Greek Septuagint
Mt	Gospel of Matthew
NAC	New American Commentary
NT	New Testament
NTS	New Testament Studies
OLD	Oxford Latin Dictionary
Oratio	Exhortation to the Greeks (Tatian)
OT	Old Testament
PG	Patrologia Graece (Migne)
PL	Patrologia Latina
Prov	Proverbs
Ps	Psalms
Quaest Hebr In Gen	Hebrew Questions on Genesis (Jerome)
Refutatio	Refutation of all Heresies (Hippolytus)
Scorpiace	Antidote for the Scorpion's Sting (Tertullian)
Sim	Similitudes (Hermas)
Song of Sol	Song of Solomon
SP	Studia Patristica
TLQ	The Lutheran Quarterly
Vg	Vulgate
Vit Mos	Life of Moses (Philo)
VL	Vetus Latina
WBC	Word Biblical Commentary
Wisdom of Sol	Wisdom of Solomon

Chapter One

Daniélou and the Angelomorphic Christology of Tertullian

Two of this study's aims are to show that (1) Tertullian's Christology contains Angelomorphic elements; (2) He does not posit a vast ontological divide (i.e. a radical distinction of being) between the pre-existent Son and the holy angels of God. This chapter will consequently examine Daniélou's two suggestions, namely, that Tertullian both rejects Angelomorphic Christology *tout court* and believes that the Son is radically distinct from the angels. We will now engage in a critical analysis of Daniélou's arguments in order to ascertain their possible historical validity. First, however, we will briefly review studies that precipitated Daniélou's investigation of Angelomorphic Christology. Of course, we do not intend for the summary presented in this study to be comprehensive or exhaustive. Its purpose is merely to provide the reader with selected background information on the subject of angelomorphism as it relates to the doctrine of Christ. One can find comprehensive summaries of Angelomorphic research in Gieschen and Carrell.[1]

A. RECENT CHRISTOLOGICAL STUDIES CONCERNING ANGELOMORPHISM

Two types of nomenclature that students of Second Temple Judaism and early Christianity have devoted a considerable amount of attention to in recent years are the linguistic formulae "angelic" and "Angelomorphic" Christology.[2] The expression angelic Christology usually refers to the doctrine that maintains Christ is an angelic being as to His nature (*ut natura*).[3] Angelomorphic Christology[4], on the other hand, proposes that the Son of God momentarily assumes the form (*morphe*) of an angel when He manifests Himself in divinely inspired visions such as those contained in the NT book of Revelation (Apocalypse 1:13–16).[5] Additionally, ancient Hebrew narratives that historically recount the awe-inspiring angelophanies of the *malak YHWH* also appear to include data that contribute to the study of Angelomorphic traditions (Genesis 16:7–14).[6] Of course, we cannot neglect the early Jewish apocalyptic or Patristic sources either. They too provide indispensable information that illumines our understanding of Christ's role as an angel qua angel.

The difference between angelic and Angelomorphic Christology seems to be one of descriptive emphasis: one model delineates the nature or essence of a certain entity (x) while the other paradigm describes a particular function of x. Scholars employ both angelic and Angelomorphic Christology to account for the otherworldly phenomena recorded in the ancient holy writings of Judaism and Christianity. However, the language "Angelomorphic Christology" has taken on greater prominence since a very controversial study appeared in the 1940s. For this reason, it is imperative that we review details concerning this much talked about work and discuss the varied responses to this study.

The terminology "angel Christology" particularly came to the fore when Martin Werner authored the book, *Die Enstehung des Dogmas*, in 1941.[7] Admittedly, scholars produced learned delineations of early angelic Christology prior to Werner's formative study.[8] Nevertheless, Werner's opus garnered especial attention by virtue of the negative scholarly response it received *in toto*. More importantly, Wilhelm Michaelis (*inter alios*) immediately criticized Werner's controversial monograph, doing so authoritatively and decisively in 1942.[9] Consequently, *Die Enstehung des Dogmas,* a publication that outlines a highly disputed form of *urchristlich* teaching, never recovered from the learned theological offensive that the notable German scholar Michaelis initiated. The scholastic world never accepted Werner's general thesis and the majority of patristic, ecclesiastical, and NT scholars continue rejecting it until this day.[10]

While most ecclesiastical historians and NT scholars believe that Michaelis and those who followed in his path soundly overturned Werner's argument concerning the ostensible angel Christology of early Christianity, we do well to remember that certain historians of dogma have expressed scholastic praise for Werner's historical presentation of Judaeo-Christian evidence that ostensibly demonstrates the existence of Primitive angelic Christology. Admittedly, scholars usually deny Werner's primary overarching thesis.[11] Nonetheless, in recent times, Charles Gieschen's magisterial study has further highlighted distinctive elements of Angelomorphic Christology from early Jewish *testimonia* that no doubt shaped and informed Primitive and postapostolic Christianity. Gieschen's painstaking examination of the issues and texts appertaining to angelic or Angelomorphic Christology suggests that

Werner's problem may have been primarily methodological, not factual *per se*. In other words, he may have claimed more than the evidence that he presented actually warranted.[12] His approach may therefore have been non-analytical.

Gieschen endeavors to avoid the trap that Werner putatively fell prey to by attempting to bracket ontological issues when he examines the antecedents of and the lines of evidence for ancient Angelomorphic traditions. How well Gieschen succeeds in this endeavor, though, is somewhat debatable.[13] At any rate, Gieschen's research in connection with Angelomorphic Christology is groundbreaking. Ergo, we deem it appropriate to evaluate the data he has compiled in his analysis of Angelomorphic texts. Although this chapter will primarily appeal to Gieschen's study, it will first review Daniélou's comments concerning the absence or presence of Angelomorphic Christology in Tertullian's literary corpus to ascertain their historical viability.

B. THE QUESTION OF ANGELOMORPHIC CHRISTOLOGY IN TERTULLIAN'S WRITINGS

Daniélou maintains that Tertullian assumes an antagonistic stance vis-à-vis "Judaeo-Christian angelology."[14] For instance, he maintains that the seminal Carthaginian thinker firmly repudiates a noted Jewish teaching that suggests the angels shared with God in creating the first man and woman at the dawn of creation (*Adv Prax* 12.2). Additionally, Daniélou argues that Tertullian rejects the supposed Judaeo-Christian concept of *potestates ianitrices*, that is, the notion that there are angels who purportedly judge the departed souls of deceased humans in the so-called hereafter.[15] With characteristic irony, Tertullian writes:

> Doubtless, when the souls have departed from their bodies, and begun to be put upon trial in the several stories of the heavens, with reference to the engagement (under which they have come to Jesus), and to be questioned about those hidden mysteries of the heretics, they must then confess before the real powers and the real men, the Teleti, to wit, and the Abascanti, and the Acineti of Valentinus![16]

It seems certain that Tertullian does not believe angels pass eternal judgment upon human souls that depart *post mortem*. Does this mean that he absolutely rejected Angelomorphic Christology or Judaic angelology, however?

In view of the foregoing quote from Tertullian's work *Scorpiace*, it seems reasonable to conclude that the Christian rhetorician from North Africa resolutely opposed all gnoseological elements that were contained in so-called Jewish Christian angelology. Nevertheless, it is also clear from a careful reading of Tertullian's writings that he does not renounce Jewish angelology *in toto*. For example, a perusal of Tertullian's well-written discourse concerning the soul reveals that he openly affirmed the existence of natality angels (a putative Second Temple Judaic notion)[17] in addition to accommodating the theory of a heavenly spirit being dutifully escorting the soul "on its journey" after death occurs:

> Undoubtedly, when the soul, by the power of death, is released from its concretion with the flesh, it is by the very release cleansed and purified. It is, moreover, certain that it escapes from the veil of the flesh into open space, to its clear, and pure, and intrinsic light and then finds itself enjoying its enfranchisement from matter, and by virtue of its liberty it recovers its divinity, as one who awakes out of sleep passes from images to verities. Then it tells out what it sees; then it exults or it fears, according as it finds what lodging is prepared for it, as soon as it sees the very angel's face, that arraigner of souls, the Mercury of the poets.[18]

It seems evident from the passage quoted above, that Tertullian does not eschew all forms of Jewish angelology. His acceptance of certain Jewish angelological constituents is also apparent from what he writes in *De Vir Vel* 7.2 regarding the angels who sinned against God by marrying attractive women in the days of Noah (Gen 6:1–4; 1 Enoch 6:1–8; 12:1–16:4; 19:1; 2 Baruch 56:12).[19] Nonetheless, Daniélou does not simply think Tertullian evinces antipathy towards Judaeo-Christianity by casting off certain vestiges of Jewish angelology: He makes the stronger contention that "Tertullian rejects all Angelomorphic Christology."[20] While Daniélou's work is certainly first-rate and quite innovative in many respects, we believe that it also contains certain problematic features with respect to Tertullian's concept of Angelomorphic Christology. We will now discuss these apparent problemata.

C. PROBLEMATA ASSOCIATED WITH DANIÉLOU'S HISTORICAL METHOD

There is one methodological difficulty that directly affects the phenomenological efficacy of Daniélou's retelling (*historia*) of Latin dogmatic history (*Dogmengeschichte*). First, it is doubtful whether Judaeo-Christianity, as delineated by Daniélou, ever truly existed: "Jewish Christianity in the early centuries was a remarkably diversified phenomenon."[21] Judaeo-Christianity was not monolithic. Therefore, we submit that one cannot facilely compartmentalize early Christianity into categories such as Daniélou employs (Jewish, Latin and Hellenistic) and expect that justice will be done to the variegated forms of Christian thought that actually obtained in antiquity.[22] The three putative types of Christianity posited by Daniélou overlap with one another and contain homogeneous features that somewhat render alleged ecclesiastical distinctions superfluous from an ontological or structural standpoint. The distinctions made by Daniélou are therefore to some extent arbitrary (it appears).[23] Hellenistic and Jewish thought were possibly interfertilized during the Second Temple period, while in the first century, the primitive *ecclesia* most certainly did not seem constituted in the way that Daniélou proposed, though we do not want to imply that Hellenism exerted a significant influence on the first century Christian assembly.

Moreover, how does one proceed to determine the essential constituents of Jewish Christianity? What doctrines, beliefs or practices enable us to label a particular religious phenomenon "Judaeo-Christianity"? Moreover, what is the chronological starting point that the historian should take into consideration when analyzing ancient Jewish Christian religious phenomena? Gieschen, though he understandably lauds Daniélou's general contributions to the field of Angelomorphic Christology, also thinks there is a slight methodological problem with his work. He believes that Daniélou's model of Judaeo-Christianity may need to be revised or nuanced in view of the criteria that he employed when assigning certain forms of Christianity to the Judaeo-Christian category.[24] However, there is yet another problematic aspect of Daniélou's approach to Angelomorphic Christology and Tertullian that we need to address.

Bray discusses a number of relevant aporias that are associated with Daniélou's general thesis.[25] He concludes that Daniélou's historical reconstruction of pre-Nicene Christianity is not wholly convincing since the historian seems to argue without sufficient warrant that Tertullian's work *Scorpiace* is dependent on *Adversus Judaeos*.[26] Furthermore, Daniélou considers the *Passio Perpetuae* a second century document.[27] This suggestion is highly unlikely, however, in view of the events that this document records. Vivia Perpetua and Felicitas of Carthage were martyrs during Septimius Severus' reign. They sacrificed their lives for the Christian faith in 202 CE.[28] The account contained in the *Passio Perpetuae*, which Tertullian possibly composed, must therefore be relating events that transpired in the third century.

Lastly, Daniélou defines early Jewish Christianity in extremely broad terms, mistakenly equating much of it with ancient Gnosticism.[29] This is undoubtedly why he appears to make a *faux pas* when arguing that Tertullian assumes a perpetual *prise de position* against Judaiam. Tertullian actually rails against certain forms of Judaism or particular gnoseological Judaic concepts, not against Judaism *simpliciter*. Daniélou's view of Tertullian's relationship with Judaism certainly plays a part in his construal of the Christology contained in *Adversus Praxean*. However, his *modus operandi* may overlook the cross-fertilization or syncretism that evidently obtained between Judaism and Hellenism during the Second Temple Period.[30]

Although Daniélou insists that Tertullian wholly expunges every element of angelomorphism from his doctrine of Christ, the "burning man" (*vir ardens*) of Carthage[31] appears to clearly depict God's pre-enfleshed Son as the Angel of the Lord (*malak YHWH*) in Adv Prax 16. The Son is appropriately called *angelus*, "For he it always was who came down to converse with men, from Adam even to the patriarchs and prophets, always from the beginning preparing beforehand in dream and in a mirror and in an enigma that course which he was going to follow to the end."[32]

One way in which Tertullian portrays Christ as an angel is by utilizing the biblical *malak YHWH* motifs. According to the Latin writer, God's pre-existent Son is an angel since He functions as the *malak YHWH* in visions, dreams and God-given enigmas.[33] He is thus the same spiritual being who appeared "in an enigma" (*in aenigmate*) to Adam, the patriarchs and the Hebrew prophets (*ab Adam usque ad patriarchas et prophetas*).[34] Indeed, Tertullian believes that the one whom Genesis portrays deambulating in the Garden of Eden about the time of evening (*Et cum audissent vocem Domini Dei deambulantis in paradiso ad auram post meridiem*) was none other than the pre-angelophanic and pre-incarnate Son of God.[35] Hence, Tertullian lucidly affirms that from the very inception of human history, God's only-begotten Son faithfully served in the capacity of the angel or messenger (*nuntius*) of *YHWH*,[36] ever communicating God's express Will while He simultaneously learned how to be a man by means of His intermittent discourse with humans (Adv Prax 16). It is apropos, therefore, that Tertullian also employs the *malak YHWH* motif in Adv Marc 2.27, writing: "Now we believe that Christ did ever act in the name of God the Father; that He actually from the beginning held intercourse with (men); actually communed with patriarchs and prophets; was the Son of the Creator; was His Word."

Contra Daniélou, there is evidently ample evidence that Tertullian mentally associated the Angel of the Lord (*malak YHWH*) with God's angelophanic Son.[37] The motifs that Tertullian utilizes thereby demonstrate that Angelomorphic themes are to be found in his anti-heretical treatises. The pre-Nicene from Carthage consistently maintains that Christ has assumed an angelic form when the Will of God deemed such an *assumptio formae angelicae* necessary. When making such observations, however, we do not mean to minimize the fact that Tertullian clearly ascribes the moniker "angel" to Christ. For instance, Tertullian applies the term "angel" to Christ in *De Carne* 14.17–20:

"Certainly he is described as the angel of great counsel, 'angel' meaning 'messenger', by a term of office, not of nature: for he was to announce to the world the Father's great project, concerned with the restitution of man."[38] Such an explicit declaration of Christ's angelhood, however, seems to be rare in the literary corpus of Tertullian. Tertullian is extremely reluctant to identify Christ as an angel. In fact, he goes to great lengths in order to stress that the Son is not an angel in the same way that Michael and Gabriel are angels. Additionally, Tertullian explicitly states that Christ is only an angel according to function and not with respect to His substance.[39] Even so, these concessions do not vitiate Tertullian's portrayal of the Son as an angel. There are manifest Angelomorphic elements contained in his writings whether he explicitly calls the Son "angel" or adeptly incorporates *malak YHWH* motifs. It thus does not seem quite accurate to maintain that Tertullian rejects all Angelomorphic Christology.

It is quite possible that Daniélou is working with a rather narrow or specialized definition of Angelomorphic Christology. If by "Angelomorphic Christology" he means a doctrine that asserts the Son is an angel as to nature or substance (*substantia*), then he is correct to contend that Tertullian rejects "all Angelomorphic Christology," for Tertullian did not believe that Christ possesses the entire complex of properties that determine angelhood.[40] Daniélou may therefore be using the nomenclature Angelomorphic Christology as defined above since he avers that "strictly Jewish Christian conceptions of Angelomorphic Christology" depict the Son as an angel according to nature and not simply as an *angelus* per his divine mission.[41] Nevertheless, it is doubtful that the usage "Angelomorphic Christology" adequately expresses the concept Tertullian denies. In fact, there is ample evidence that both Angelomorphic motifs and language are contained in his works. It would consequently be preferable to say that Tertullian does not affirm angelic Christology, that is, the theological doctrine posited by Werner which insists that Christ has an angelic nature or possesses the entire set of properties that ontologically constitute an angelic being.

The criticisms directed toward Daniélou in this study result from what appears to be evident semiotic imprecision on his part. We must nuance Daniélou's observations regarding Tertullian's view of Angelomorphic Christology in order to delineate satisfactorily the ancient apologist's doctrine of Christ's person and work. There is good reason to believe that Tertullian does not reject "all Angelomorphic Christology."[42] Even when he is disinclined to characterize Christ as an angel, we think that the main argument presented in this study accounts for such times of reticence. Accordingly, we contend that there are discernible traces of Angelomorphic Christology in the writings of the ancient Carthaginian. Gieschen evidently concurs with this assessment since he writes:

> The idea that all visible manifestations of God are the Son had a pervasive influence on many of the church's leading exegetes. Tertullian, whose writings date from ca. 193–220 CE, is also guided by this principle. He, too, assigns all judgment and revelatory activity, including that carried out by the Angel of the Lord, to the Son.[43]

While he acknowledges that Angelomorphic Christology is contained in Tertullian's theological treatises, Gieschen is quick to point out that former's terminology does not mean the apologist believes Christ possesses an angelic nature. On the other hand, Justin Martyr evidently did affirm that Christ is an angel *per substantiam* or κατ' ουσιαν: "But both Him, and the Son (who came forth from Him and taught us these things, and the host of the other good angels who follow and are made like to Him), and the prophetic Spirit, we worship and adore, knowing them in reason and truth, and declaring without grudging to every one who wishes to learn, as we have been taught (1 *Apology* 6.1–2). Gieschen explains the famed Justinian passage as follows:

What is striking about this text is both Justin's acknowledgement that angels are made like Christ (i.e., of the same nature) and the inclusion of angels as receiving 'worship and adoration' (sebomeqa kai proskunoumen) in a sequence after the Father and the Son and before the (prophetic) Spirit.[44]

Gieschen suggests that Tertullian may be reacting to Justin's distinctive form of Angelomorphic Christology by stressing Christ's function as an angel, in contrast to Justin's doctrine of Christ, which perceives and posits a nexus between the Son and God's "good angels."[45] Nonetheless, there is reason to believe that other factors govern Tertullian's emphasis on Christ's function (His *ex officio* status) as an angel over against His possessing an angelic nature in the *modus* of Michael and Gabriel. We will review these factors later. For now, it seems that the following conclusions are tentatively warranted.

The pioneer of Latin Christianity unequivocally writes that Christ is not an angel with respect to His nature but only such in an *ex officio* manner (*De Carne* 14.17–20). Such denial or reluctance passages in the Tertullian corpus do not undermine the fact that vestiges of Angelomorphic Christology do appear in these writings. Therefore, while the noted pre-Nicene's doctrine of Christ is admittedly complex and resists reductionistic explanations, it is sufficient to note that Daniélou's argument regarding the absence of Angelomorphic Christology in Tertullian's work simply will not hold up under scrutiny. It is much better to say that Tertullian does not believe the Son is an angel in the manner of Gabriel and Michael than to maintain that he rejects Angelomorphic Christology *ex toto*.[46] Accordingly, let us now discuss a second claim of Daniélou that appertains to our study. This contention involves the ontological relationship between Christ and the angels.

D. THE ONTOLOGICAL CHASM AND TERTULLIAN'S ANGELOMORPHIC AVERSION

Having demonstrated that Daniélou appears to be employing the expression "Angelomorphic Christology" catachrestically, this study will now utilize the concept, "angelic Christology" to describe the doctrine that Daniélou contends Tertullian repudiates. Having established that the pre-Nicene apologist is not averse to all forms of Angelomorphic Christology, however, we will now explore whether his rejection of what is, in reality, angelic Christology stems from elevated ontological notions concerning the Son of God.

We must admit that Tertullian does not prefer to identify Christ as an angel. Furthermore, when he does use *angelus* with reference to the Son, he overtly declares that the Son is only an angel in the sense that He is a messenger (*nuntius*) for the Father. That is, Christ is not an angel according to His nature (*ut natura*). Nevertheless, we do well to ask why the Latin apologist *par excellence* apparently does not attribute angelic properties to the preeminent Son of God. Why is he so hesitant to impute angelhood to the Son? In the attempt to obtain an answer to such queries, we will now review Daniélou's discussion of *Adv Prax* 3.4–10 and analyze the putative ontological divide that he proposes between Christ and the angels.

E. CRITIQUING DANIÉLOU'S ANALYSIS OF ADVERSUS PRAXEAN 3

Tertullian allegedly rejects all Angelomorphic Christology since he is supposed to believe there is a "radical distinction" between God's ministering angels (*igitur si et monarchia divina per tot legiones et exercitus angelorum administratur sicut scriptum est*)[47] and the two prolations of the Trinitarian Godhead that Tertullian teaches share one divine substance (*tres personae una substantia*) with the Father.[48] The pre-Nicene purportedly makes a distinction between Christ, the Holy Spirit and the angels for two primary reasons: (1) The angels are not members of God's monarchy, which is exclusively constituted of the *tres personae*; (2) Tertullian believes the angels are not consubstantial with the Father.

Daniélou first appeals to *Adv Prax* 3.4–10 in order to demonstrate the marked differentiation that he thinks Tertullian makes between the innumerable holy angels of the Christian deity and the two divine emanations of the

Trinity (i.e. the Son and Holy Spirit). *Adv Prax* 3.4–10 states that the angels administer God's single rule (*monarchia*) but do not thereby destroy it.[49] Furthermore, this textual unit may indicate that the angels are not consubstantial (*consubstantialis*) with the Father. In fact, they are possibly alienated from His very substance since Tertullian writes:

> Therefore if also the divine monarchy is administered by the agency of so many legions and hosts of angels (as it is written, Ten thousand times ten thousand stood before him and thousand thousands ministered unto him), yet has not ceased to belong to one, so as to cease to be a monarchy because it has for its provincial governors so many thousand authorities, how should God be thought, in the Son and in the Holy Spirit occupying second and third place, while they are to such a degree conjoint of the Father's substance, to experience a division and a dispersion such as he does not experience in the plurality of all those angels, alien as they are from the Father's substance.[50]

The rhetorical period (periodov) constructed in the previously quoted passage is somewhat protracted and relatively complicated. Nevertheless, the general thesis communicated by this text is for the most part unambiguous.

Although the divine monarchy (*monarchia*) is the sole government (single empire) of God, the Almighty Sovereign permits His heavenly subordinates (i.e. the angels) to administer the cosmic Kingdom in His behalf without the said rule of deity suffering any monarchical diminution whatsoever. Tertullian portrays God's sovereign willingness to delegate authority to creaturely essences in the following terms: "The divine monarchy is administered by the agency of so many legions and hosts of angels (as it is written, Ten thousand times ten thousand stood before him and thousand thousands ministered unto him), yet has not ceased to belong to one."[51]

The comments of the ancient Carthaginian further reveal why Jesus of Nazareth could speak of summoning twelve legions of angels (a multitude of holy spirit creatures) who possessed the God-given puissance to deliver God's enfleshed Son from the life-threatening thralls of His *prima facie* formidable opponents. As shown in *Adv Prax* 3.4–10, Tertullian affirms that there are myriads of celestial beings that attend God the Father's heavenly throne. Consequently, the Son "ordains for his disciples a kingdom even as He says one has been ordained for Him by His Father: and He has power to ask His Father for legions of angels to help Him, if He wished."[52] These angels, Jesus of Nazareth believed, comprise the heavenly army of *YHWH* often referred to in the Hebrew Scriptures by means of the formula *YHWH Sabaoth* (Ps 68:17).[53] They are evidently akin to mighty winds (πνευματα) or flaming fires, figuratively speaking (Heb 1:7, 14). Such ones fittingly represent God's *monarchia* because of divine *permissio*.

Although they administer the sole rule of God with all due care and dilligence, the incalculable legions of supernal beings, whom both Jesus and Tertullian allude to, never cause any dissolution to the suzerainty of God. They are concomitantly God's servants (*exercitus angelorum administretur*) and spiritual sons.[54] God the Father has graciously allowed His "family connections" (*pignora*)[55] or sons to administer His supreme monarchical arrangement in the capacity of submissive heavenly officials (*officiales*).[56] This arrangement in nowise impugns or diminishes the divine unicity, as Tertullian so avidly contends.

In order to substantiate His contention scripturally, Tertullian recalls the words of the prophet Daniel: "As it is written, Ten thousand times ten thousand stood before him and thousand thousands ministered to him" (*sicut scriptum est, Milies centies centena milia adsistebant ei*). Daniel, similar to the author of Apocalypse (Apoc 7:11–12), vividly depicts myriads upon myriads of angels surrounding the awe-inspiring throne of The Most High (*altissimus*) in a resplendent deific vision (Dan 7:10).[57] Yet, the thousands of angels that John or Daniel behold never threaten the sole cosmic rule of Almighty God. Tertullian thus inquires of Praxeas: "Do you account provinces and family connections and officials and the very forces and the whole trappings of empire to be the overthrow of it? You are wrong if you do" (*membra et pignora et instrumenta et ipsam vim ac totum censum monarchiae eversionem deputas eius? Non recte*).[58] A fortiori, the angels (Tertullian reasons) uphold God's supreme empire as loyal servants and sons ("family connections"). Their task is simply to administer God's monarchy as He wills without imperiling His divine sovereignty or unicity.

Basing our thoughts on the language used in *Adv Prax* 3.4–10, we think it is appropriate to conclude that Tertullian affirmed that the countless subordinate divine beings (= the angels) evidently existing in the heavens of God's presence are actually part of God's monarchy: they serve as eminent administrators of the divine Kingdom. However, Daniélou argues that Tertullian radically distinguishes these angelic ministers of God from the only begotten Son of the Most High deity and the Holy Spirit, who (according to Tertullian) respectively occupy second and third place in the Godhead (*videatur in filio et in spiritu sancto secundum et tertium sortitis locum*).[59] What are we to make of his argument in view of this discussion concerning *Adv Prax* 3.4–10? What are Daniélou's reasons for epistemically excluding the angels from God's *monarchia*?

While the Son and Spirit of holiness (according to Tertullian) share the Father's *substantia* (being extensions thereof),[60] Daniélou observes that the angels are aliens of the Father's substance (*alienorum a substantia patris*).[61] Consequently, he thinks we have one line of evidence that indicates Tertullian makes a marked ontological differentiation between the angels and God's pre-eminent Son and Holy Spirit. These arguments do not necessarily convince the present writer, however, for the following three reasons:

(1) As we have implied above, *Adv Prax* 3.4–10 suggests that the celestial preternatural beings that attend God's throne are actually members of God's *monarchia*. In company with God's Son and Holy Spirit, the angels constitute part of the divine monarchy. Tertullian indicates that the holy angels serve as eminent dignitaries ("provincial governors") of the divine Kingdom. The supreme kingdom "has for its provincial governors so many thousand authorities" (*quia per tant milia virtutum procuratur*) since deific subordinate spirit beings share in its benevolent sphere of influence.[62] In this exalted capacity, they faithfully oversee the single rule (*monarchia*) of the supreme Monarch, being an integral part of His peerless empire. Tertullian in fact attributes a highly exalted position to the angels in relation to deity, for he thinks that the "angels rank next to God."[63]

(2) The reading, *alienorum a substantia patris*, is possibly a corrupt one.[64] Evans himself only essays it as a possible reconstructed lection. Consequently, we do not think that Daniélou's contention is ultimately probative. Tertullian may or may not think the angels are consubstantial (*consubstantialis*) with the Father. However, it does not seem that one can dogmatically appeal to *Adv Prax* 3.4–10 to establish either view. The reading *alienorum a substantia patris* may very well be inauthentic since later in Tertullian's treatise, he insists that God has created humans from His very substance. Humanity is has thus been made in the *imago Dei*.[65] Why then, cannot the angels who evidently surpass human beings in power and strength (2 Pet 2:11) also share in or originate from God's substance? The germane and important point here, however, is what Tertullian thought about the relationship between the angels and God's *substantia*. It seems well within the realm of possibility that Tertullian viewed the angels as extensions of God's substance.

(3) A careful evaluation of Tertullian's literary corpus demonstrates that he not only applied Ps 8:5 to the incarnate Son of God, but he also assigns this text to the minoration of the Son within the Godhead.[66] That is, Tertullian believes that the pre-incarnate and pre-angelophanic Son of God was actually lower than the angels before He became a man or manifested Himself to the prophets and patriarchs via visions and enigmata since He experienced a perfect temporal birth in heaven (*nativitas perfecta*) before experiencing an earthly *nativitas* through the Virgin Mary. We therefore submit that Tertullian actually believes the Son *qua* Son was lower than

God's holy angels prior to His enfleshment. This is one of the main reasons that Tertullian is not inclined to attribute angelic properties to the Son. Ultimately we contend that a sustained analysis of *Adversus Praxean* will buttress the suggestion put forth here. But now that we have evaluated Daniélou's view, thereby setting the stage for our subsequent treatment of Tertullian's work, we will examine how the pre-Nicenes employ Ps 8:5.

NOTES

1. Peter R. Carrell, *Jesus and the Angels: Angelology and the Christology of the Apocalypse of John* (Cambridge: Cambridge University Press, 1997).

2. Christology is the doctrine of Christ. The term thus refers to the theological dogma that systematically focuses on the person and work of the one whom Christians universally consider the elect and divine Messiah of God. One of the most influential Christologies in church history is the doctrine of Christ carefully worked out by Tertullian of Carthage in the third century.

3. We say "usually" since scholars such as Hannah employ the terminology "angel christology" to describe all Christologies that have been markedly influenced "by angelological ideas." See Hannah, *Michael and Christ*, 12–13, wherein he notes that angelic Christology particularly "defines Christ as an angelic being," however.

4. While relating that Daniélou is evidently the first writer to use the terminology, "Angelomorphic Christology," Hannah also informs his readers that this type of Christology is "phenomenological." That is, "It refers only to visual portrayals of Christ in the form of an angel." See *Michael and Christ*, 13. The emphasis here is on Christ being depicted in terms of His angelic μορφη. He therefore manifests himself with the external appearance of an angel although he may not be an angel in an ontological sense. For more information on how the early church fathers use μορφη, *vide* Lampe. One will find an extended definition of Angelomorphic Christology in Gieschen, *Angelomorphic Christology*, 28–29.

5. Stuckenbruck provides evidence for Angelomorphic elements in Apoc 1:13–16. See *Angel Veneration*, 211–213.

6. It is difficult to improve on Carrell's precise definition of angels. He describes them as "heavenly beings distinct from God and human beings, who exist to serve Deity as messengers, as the heavenly congregation in worship, and as agents of the divine will fulfilling a variety of other functions," in *Jesus and the Angels*, 14. Angelology thus involves propositional declarations concerning angels and it systematically treats the heavenly spirit creatures that dutifully minister to Almighty God.

7. *The Formation of Christian Dogma: An Historical Study of Its Problem*, trans. S. G. F. Brandon (London: Black, 1957).

8. G. H. Dix wrote two articles contending that primitive Christology originated from Judaism's notion of the *malak YHWH* and Son of Man concepts. These articles

were respectively published in 1925 and 1927. The details are contained in Hannah, *Michael and Christ*, 3.

9. Hannah recounts how scholars replied to Werner's study in a "swift and decisive" fashion. For instance, Joseph Barbel presented a critique of Werner's thesis in 1941. Then came Michaelis' *Zur Engelchristologie im Urchristentum: Abbau der Konstruktion Martin Werners*. Barbel lauded the evidence that Werner marshaled, although he did not think that the primitive community of faith adhered to an authentic angel Christology. See Hannah, *Michael and Christ*, 4–5.

Werner himself seems to consider Barbel's study more significant than Michaelis'. He certainly spends more time replying to the former than to the latter in his second edition of *Formation*. Interestingly, Barbel thought that the pre-Nicenes held to a form of angel Christology but he did not find evidence for its existence in the primitive congregation. See *Michael and Christ*, 4ff.

10. Carrell, *Jesus and the Angels*, 3.

11. Hannah, *Michael and Christ*, 5.

12. Gieschen considers Werner's documentation for the existence of first century angelic Christology (the doctrine that Christ is a created angel) "meager." See *Angelomorphic Christology*, 13. Martin Hengel offers a similar analysis: "At any rate, in his great work *The Formation of Christian Dogma*, Martin Werner much exaggerated the role of 'angel Christology' in early Christianity (*Martin Werner hat auf jeden Fall in seinem grossen Werk 'Die Enstehung des christlichen Dogmas' die Rolle der 'Engelchristologie' für das frühe Christentum weit überschätzt.*" See *Der Sohn Gottes: Die Enstehung der Christologie und die judisch-hellenistische Religionsgeschichte* (Tübingen: JCB Mohr [Paul Siebeck], 1975), 131; *The Son of God: The Origin of Christology and the History of Jewish-Hellenistic Religion* (London: SCM Press, 1976), 85.

13. Gieschen believes that ontological concerns (questions concerning the being of Christ) have "inhibited" Angelomorphic studies undertaken in the past. He proposes that we should now ask another question in place of the ontological ones, namely, "Where and how did early Christians use the variegated angelomorphic traditions from the OT and other sources to express their Christology?" Consult *Angelomorphic Christology*, 349. Gieschen's new formulation of the Angelomorphic question is designed to show that Angelomorphic traditions significantly influenced early Christology *qua* high Christology. He further maintains that traditions portraying Christ as the visible manifestation of God (the *malak YHWH*) actually paved the way for later Christological affirmations such as "Jesus is Lord" (1 Cor 12:3) or *YHWH*. See ibid. 350. While he tries to downplay questions concerning the being of Christ in his study, it is evident that Gieschen espouses a high Christology, linking the Son in his role as angel with a visible manifestation of *YHWH*.

14. Danielou, *History of Early Church Doctrine*, 3:142.

15. Ibid. Tertullian might have based his animus for this doctrine on what we read in Hermas, *Visions* 1.1; 3.2; 4.1 and *Sim* 9.2 (written ca. 145).

16. *Scorpiace* 10.6–7.

17. *De Anima* 37.1–2 reads: "Now the entire process of sowing, forming, and completing the human embryo in the womb is no doubt regulated by some power, which

ministers herein to the will of God, whatever may be the method which it is appointed to employ. Even the superstition of Rome, by carefully attending to these points, imagined the goddess Alemona to nourish the foetus in the womb; as well as (the goddesses) Nona and Decima, called after the most critical months of gestation; and Partula, to manage and direct parturition; and Lucina, to bring the child to the birth and light of day. We, on our part, believe the angels to officiate herein for God. The embryo therefore becomes a human being in the womb from the moment that its form is completed" (Omnem autem hominis in utero serendi struendi fingendi paraturam/ aliqua utique potestas divinae voluntatis ministra modulatur, quamcumque illam rationem agitare sortita. Haec aestimando etiam superstitio Romana deam finxit Alemonam alendi in utero fetus et Nonam et Decimam a sollicitioribus mensibus et Partulam, quae partum gubernet, et Lucinam, quae producat in lucem. Nos officia divina angelos credimus. Ex eo igitur fetus in utero homo, a quo forma completa est). Jan H. Waszink, *De Anima* (Amsterdam: Meulenhoff, 1947).

18. Waszink, *De Anima* 53.6. Procul dubio cum vi mortis exprimitur de concretione carnis et ipsa expressione colatur, certe de oppanso corporis erumpit in apertum ad meram et puram et suam lucem, statim semetipsam in expeditione substantiae recognoscit et in divinitatem ipsa libertate resipiscit, ut de somnio emergens ab imaginibus ad veritates. Tunc et enuntiat et videt, tunc exultat aut trepidat, prout paraturam devorsorii sui sentit, de ipsius statim angeli facie, evocatoris animarum, Mercurii poetarum. Compare Lk 16:22.

19. See Norman Hillyer. *1 and 2 Peter, Jude*. New International Biblical Commentary (Peabody: Hendrickson, 1992), 118.

20. Daniélou, *History of Early Christian Doctrine*, 3:149.

21. Bart Ehrman, *The Orthodox Corruption of Scripture: The Effect of Early Christological Controversies on the Text of the New Testament* (Oxford: Oxford University Press, 1993), 50–51.

22. See R. A. Kraft. "In Search of 'Jewish Christianity' and its 'Theology': Problems of Definition and Methodology," *Recherches de Science Religieuse* 60 (1972) 81–92.

23. John A. Baker (editor and translator of Daniélou's *magnum opus*) recognizes this complication with the late historian's paradigm, while still affirming the overall value of his historical account. See *History of Early Christian Doctrine*, 3:469–477.

24. Gieschen, *Angelomorphic Christology*, 15.

25. Bray, *Holiness and the Will of God*, 131–132.

26. Ibid.

27. ibid. Cf. Danielou, *History of Early Christian Doctrine*, 3:18.

28. See Henry Chadwick. *The Early Church: The Story of Emergent Christianity from the Apostolic Age to the Dividing of the Ways between the Greek East and the Latin West* (London: Penguin, 1993), 91.

29. Bray, *Holiness and the Will of God*, 132. Despite the criticisms leveled here, we concur with Kearsley who acknowledges the impressive array of data that Daniélou amasses to highlight specific characteristics of Jewish Christianity. See Kearsley, *Tertullian's Theology*, 4.

30. Martin Hengel, *Judaism and Hellenism: Studies in their Encounter in Palestine during the Early Hellenistic Period*, 2 vols. (London: SCM Press, 1974). For an

opposing viewpoint, see L. H. Feldman. "Hengel's *Judaism and Hellenism* in Retrospect," *JBL* 96 (1977): 371–382.

31. Jerome, *Ep.* 84.2.

32. *Adv Prax* 16.28–32: "Ipse enim et ad humana semper colloquia descendit, ab Adam usque ad patriarchas et prophetas, in visione in somnio in speculo in aenigmate ordinem suum praestruens ab initio semper quem erat persecuturus in finem."

33. Margaret Barker proposes that first century Palestinian Jews clung to a putative OT worldview (*Weltanschauung*) that conceived the *malak YHWH* in terms of a son of God who has the potential to temporarily embody himself in human form. She writes concerning Christ: "It was as a manifestation of Yahweh, the Son of God, that Jesus was acknowledged as Son of God, Messiah and Lord." See *The Great Angel: A Study of Israel's Second God* (London: SPCK, 1992), 3. Jewish monotheism, as Barker understands it, did not prevent *El Elyon* from having a number of angelic sons, one of whom served as a visible manifestation of *YHWH* in the capacity of *malak YHWH*.

34. *Adv Prax* 16.

35. Gen 3:8 (Vg).

36. *De Carne* 14.5.

37. This was actually a common attribution made by the pre-Nicenes. See Basil Studer, *Trinity and Incarnation* (Collegeville: Liturgical Press, 1993), 37–41.

38. "Dictus est quidem magni consilii angelus, id est nuntius, officii non naturae vocabulo: magnum enim cogitatum patris, super hominis scilicet restitutionem, adnuntiaturus saeculo erat."

39. Gieschen, *Angelomorphic Christology*, 193.

40. The Jewish Christian delineation of Angelomorphic Christology is said to be accomplished by means of angelic imagery since it evidently depicts the Son as an angel in substance or in his very eternal being.

The present writer's comment about angelic properties assumes that there are truly mind-independent spiritual entities that possess certain objective (mind-independent) properties (qualities, characteristics and attributes) that allow such spiritual entities in relation to collectively belong to the class of being that some call angels. An extensive discussion of properties *simpliciter* is outside the bounds of this study. Suffice it to say that a sophicated account of a priori contingent (*per accidens*) properties and a posteriori necessary properties appears in Saul Kripke's *Naming and Necessity* (Cambridge: Harvard University Press, 1972, 1980), 106–34.

41. Daniélou, *History of Early Church Doctrine*, 1:146.

42. Carrell is a little more cautious in his wording. He notes that Tertullian "was suspicious of angel Christology" although he calls Christ "the Angel of Great Counsel" (*Jesus and the Angels*, 101).

43. *Angelomorphic Christology*, 193–194.

44. Ibid.

45. Note Talbert's discussion concerning the incorporation of the *malak YHWH* concept in Tertullian and his "distaste" for the "docetic implications" of Angelomorphic Christology. See C. H. Talbert, "The Myth of the Descending-Ascending Redeemer in Mediterranean Antiquity," *NTS* 22 (1976): 418–440.

46. Carrell, *Jesus and the Angels*, 101.

47. *Adv Prax* 3.35ff: "Therefore if also the divine monarchy is administered by the agency of so many legions and host of angels, as it is written."

48. J. Daniélou, *History of Early Church Doctrine*, 3:149–150. Tertullian himself (*Adv Prax* 2.3–7) writes that the *personae trinitatis* are three as regards sequence, aspect, and manifestation of power, yet one with respect to quality, power and substance. The three sequences, aspects and manifestations of power are "reckoned out in the name of three persons" (tres autem non statu sed gradu, nec substantia sed forma, nec potestate sed specie, unius autem substantiae et unius status et unius postestatis, quia unus deus ex quo et gradus isti et formae et species in nomine patris et filii et spiritus sancti deputantur).

49. Moltmann's *Trinity and the Kingdom*, 130–134 contains pertinent information concerning the history of the term *monarchia*. Moltmann points out that this "curious hellenistic word-formation" is a Greek compound of μονας and μία αρχη. Moltmann consequently states that this term originates with Pythagorean terminology used in Alexandria. He observes that we also find the concept of God's *monarchia* in Philo, Justin, and Tatian where it respectively refers to God's lordship (Justin), the "monarchical constitution" of the cosmos (Tatian) or God's universal sovereignty (Philo). Tertullian appears to employ the signifier in order to reference God's supreme empire or rule (130–131). Moltmann argues that the pre-Nicenes thus replace the biblical concept of βασίλεια with what he calls, "an uncommonly seductive religious-political ideology" (131).

50. *Adv Prax* 3: "Igitur si et monarchia divina per toto legiones et exercitus angelorum administretur sicut scriptum est, Milies centies centena milia adsistebant ei, nec ideo unius esse desiit, ut desinat monarchia esse quia per tanta milia virtutum procuratur, Quale est ut deus divisionem et dispersionem pati videatur in filio et in spiritu sancto secundum et tertium sortitis locum, tam consortibus substantiae patris, quas non patitur in tot angelorum numero et quidem tam alienorum a substantia patris."

51. Ibid.

52. *Adv Prax* 26.11–14: "Disponens regnum discipulis quomodo et sibi dispositum dicit a patre, habens potestatem legiones angelorum postulandi ad auxilium a patre si vellet."

53. The NT Epistle of James also appears to employ this expression in 5:4 of that work. For details of James' use of the Hebraic formula, see Martin Dibelius, *James: A Commentary on the Epistle of James*, rev. Heinrich Greenven, ed. Helmut Koester (Philadelphia: Fortress Press, 1976).

54. *Adv Marc* 5.18.14. Tertullian identifies the "sons of God" in Gen 6 as angels (*De Idolatria* 9). Reference *De Virg* 7.2; 11.2. Athenagoras also believes the angels are "ministers" who, along with the Father, Son and Holy Spirit, are the subjects of Christian *theologia* (*Leg pro* 10). This functional identification evidently follows that utilized elsewhere in the NT (Heb 1:14; Rev 22:9) and Philo. Crehan however stresses that Athenagoras did not necessarily copy Philo in this regard in *Presbeia peri Christianon*, trans. and annot. Joseph Hugh Crehan, Westminster: Newman Press and London: Longmans and Green, 1956), 134.

55. E. Evans writes that the *pignora* referenced by Tertullian are sons of the Emperor. This is another point indicating that Tertullian believes the angels possibly share the substance of the Father and are actually part of His monarchy, for they are His sons.

56. *Adv Prax* 3.4.

57. See S. M. Olyan, *A Thousands Thousands Served Him: Exegesis and the Naming of Angels in Ancient Judaism* (Tubingen: J.C.B. Mohr [Paul Siebeck], 1993).

58. *Adv Prax* 3.4. Clement of Rome comments on Daniel 7:10 as follows: "Let our glorying and our confidence be in him; let us submit ourselves to his will; let us consider the whole multitude of his angels, how they stand by and serve his will. For the scripture says, Ten thousand times ten thousand stood beside him, and thousands of thousands served him; and they cried, Holy, holy, holy Lord of Sabaoth! All creation is full of his glory" (1 Clement 34.5–6).

59. *Adv Prax* 3.6.

60. Ibid. 8. George C. Stead, in his magisterial study concerning the notion of divine substance, points out that Tertullian does not hesitate to apply *substantia* to God. He notes that Tertullian uses *substantia* in *Adv Prax* 9 to describe uncreated *spiritus*, which is differentiated from created finite *spiritus* by its inherent "purity, subtlety and power, which was at first concentrated in the Father, then distributed to the Son and Spirit," see *Divine Substance* (Oxford: Clarendon Press, 1977), 161.

61. *Adv Prax* 3.8–9. Kearsley concurs with Daniélou's reading of this text. He writes that Tertullian affirms: "The Son and Holy Spirit (*Adv Prax* 3) enjoy the status of equal possessors (*consortes*) in the substance of the Father (*substantiae patris*) and not mere sharers (*participes*). By contrast, Tertullian supposedly pegs the angels as alien to the Father's substance (*alienorum a substantia patris*)." See *Tertullian's Theology*, 124. E. Osborn offers a similar analysis of Tertullian's Christology with these vivid statements: "God delegates authority to the angels; but each member of the trinity possesses *without limit* the family property. The father communicates all that he has to Son and Spirit, so that they too are omnipotent (Prax. 7.3)," see *Tertullian: First Theologian of the West* (Cambridge: Cambridge University Press, 1997), 131.

62. *Adv Prax* 3.4–5.

63. *De Res* 5.2; CCSL 2:926. *Angelos post deum novimus*. Translation found in Pelikan, *The Christian Tradition*, 1:197.

64. Aemilii Kroymann records the following textual information for Adv Prax 3.4ff: "*et quidem tam <alienorum>* Gel: *et quidem tam* PMF, *et quid?* Demta Eng, *ecquid nata*. Oehlerus. See *Corpus Scriptorum Ecclesiasticorum Latinorum Editum Consililio Et Impensis. Tertullian's Opera Ex Recensione*, vol. 47 (Vienna, 1906).

65. *Adv Prax* 5.

66. After a brief overview of how Tertullian interprets Ps 8:5 in other passages, Evans concludes: "The present passage [*Adv Prax* 9] therefore stands alone in regarding the minoration as the subordination of the Son to the Father within the Godhead" (E. Evans, *Adversus Praxean*, 248).

Chapter Two

The Exegesis of Psalm 8:5 in the Pre-Nicenes

This chapter will review the pre-Nicene exegesis of Ps 8:5. However, the early patristic interpretation of this biblical text did not occur *in vacuo*. Accordingly, Colish's observation rega rding Tertullian applies to each ante-Nicene theologian: "His thought must thus be understood in its particular historical, cultural, and existential setting."[1]

With Colish's words in mind, we will not simply examine how the pre-Nicene writers (including Tertullian) exegeted Ps 8:5; this examination of pre-Nicene exegesis will also take the life situation or vital context (*Sitz im Leben*) of select pre-Nicenes into consideration. It will investigate how writers preceding 325 CE understood the OT saying concerning the Son of Man becoming lower than the angels. Such an approach will necessitate the inclusion of a brief overview of Gnosticism since this influential amalgam of philosophico-religious ideas often precipitated scriptural explanations put forth by Tertullian or other anti-Gnostic theologians, who did their utmost to counter what they considered heretical deviations from the Christian faith. Additionally, it is imperative to review the orthodox response that anti-Gnostic writers produced in defense of historical Christianity. Only after reviewing Gnosticism, the orthodox response to this phenomenon and providing a much needed existential and cultural context for Tertullian's interpretation of Ps 8:5 will we then demonstrate how the pre-Nicenes understood the pivotal hymnodic text found in the Psalms.

A. OVERVIEW OF GNOSTICISM

The term "Gnosticism" refers to an assortment of "religious systems and ideas" that evidently thrived from the first century CE onward[2] with some forms of the movement actually surviving until the medieval period.[3] These variegated religious systems and concepts[4] were "both highly syncretistic and contemplative" in that they extracted speculative elements from diverse Jewish and pagan religio-philosophical sources[5] while promoting the notion that humankind, though provisionally subsisting in a state of spiritual obscurity, is still capable of attaining psychic liberation through the personal acquisition of γνοσις.[6]

Gnosticism posited the existence of divine aeons that putatively emanated from ungenerated Silence. For certain Gnostics, God as Silence *qua* Silence was the ineffable and incomprehensible "perfect, preexistent aeon, dwelling in the invisible and unnamable elevations."[7] Therefore, Silence functioned as the "prebeginning and forefather and depth" or "deep solitude for infinite aeons."[8] However, Pelikan also suggests that Valentinus possibly considered "depth" a deific attribute as opposed to a differentiable hypostatic divine entity related to Silence. Earlier Valentinians thus maintained that the aeons were essentially prolations "immanent with God."[9] Conversely, the Valentinian theologian named Ptolemy taught that the aeons were emanations from the "divine substance, subsisting coordinately and coeternally with deity."[10]

Dualistic and anti-worldly tendencies were also characteristic features of Gnosticism.[11] One understandable reason for the Gnostics' anti-cosmic demeanor was the plenitude of evil that the Gnostics, much like some modern theoreticians, astutely observed in the cosmos.[12] Therefore, we will now discuss the manner in which these speculative movements or speculative movement attempted to resolve the logical problem of evil.[13] In doing so, we will primarily focus on Valentinian ontology and Christology.

B. VALENTINIAN ONTOLOGY AND CHRISTOLOGY

Valentinus (ca. 140 CE) was originally a renowned member of the catholic community located in Rome.[14] Epiphanius reports that Valentinus arrived from Egypt after he received a quality education in the intellectual polis, Alexandria. The celebrated Gnostic supposedly parted ways with the church because the professed *ecclesia Christi* did not appoint him to the office of bishop (επισκοπος). Unfortunately, we only possess fragments of Valentinus' literary corpus and must therefore piece together his ontology (theory of being), Christology and the account of his alleged ecclesiastical defection from the resources available to us.

Elaine Pagels does not seem to believe that Valentinus deserted the church. Rather, she concludes that the story is an unhistorical fiction possibly perpetuated by zealous heresiologists such as Tertullian. Tertullian relates that

Valentinus became disgruntled when he was not appointed bishop of Rome. Nevertheless, historians usually discount his story for two reasons: (1) The characteristically rhetorical nature of polemic writings; (2) Historically, the orthodox seem to have parted ways with the Gnostics rather than the Gnostics separating from those who claimed to uphold historical Christianity. In any event, Tertullian's version of the evident Valentinian departure from the church does shed light on the nature of orthodoxy's general response to Gnosticism.[15]

Despite the partial nature of the historical evidence, it seems we may justly infer that Valentinus believed God created the first man Adam in accordance with a "heavenly model of the angels."[16] Valentinus also taught that Jesus only appeared to be human, but did not really assimilate the food that He reportedly ingested or the drink He purportedly imbibed during the period of His earthly enfleshment. According to Irenaeus, Valentinus also espoused the notion of a pljrwma consisting of thirty supernal aeons ordered in fifteen pairs called syzygies,[17] which included a maternal figure named *Sophia* that supposedly produced the Christ as well as the Creator (δημιυργος) of the material order.[18]

Frend argues that the following description typifies Valentinian Gnosticism: God is one, transcendent, incomprehensible and originates from the Depth (βυθος) or Primal Cause.[19] Depth (the absolute Father) brings forth Silence (Σιγετα); consequently, the two aforementioned metaphysical principles, Depth and Silence, then prolate Understanding (Νους) and Truth (Αληθεια). Altogether, thirty aeons gradually proceed or emanate, with some pleromatic entities being masculine and others feminine in nature. These prolations (i.e. emanations) collectively constitute the hidden πληρωμα (fullness of divine powers) of Gnosticism. The definitive aeon in the πληρωμα is Sophia who lapses "into the darkness of despair," and gives birth to a "malformed infant" named Ialdabaoth ("Child of Chaos").[20] The material cosmos ulteriorly derives its existence from this chaotic fallen deity otherwise known as the Demiurge. An intra-pleromatic conflict (αγων) ultimately ensues between Sophia and Ialdabaoth that Valentinus thinks is the etiological basis for the concomitant existence of good and evil.[21] Nonetheless, since cosmological evil (in a moral and natural sense)[22] is prevalent, the Gnostics argue that Sophia dispatched a Savior (Jesus) to redeem those who come to know themselves (γνωσι σεαυτου) through the medium of γνωσις θεου.

Γνωσις θεου (knowledge of God) is mystical or intuitive awareness: a "direct beholding of the divine reality" that functions as "an earnest of the consummation to come."[23] Gilbert Murray points out that γνωσις θεου "is not a mere intellectual knowledge. It is a complete union, a merging of beings."[24] Such mystical self-knowledge is the channel of salvation for the Gnostic.

Knowledge of the god within (i.e. the divine) liberates the initiate's soul from the defective fleshly body that is composed of evil or corrupted matter (ὕλη). This theme was repeatedly emphasized in the mythic soteriology of Gnosticism. By thus intermingling the motif of γνωσις θεου with its message of spiritual liberation, the Gnostic gospel attempted to rouse somnolent souls from slumber to an elevated state of wakeful existence.[25] Ultimately, however, orthodox believers in Jesus Christ concluded that the Gnostic approach was an unviable one.

In the Gnostic cosmological myth, Sophia is temporarily expelled from the locus of divine plentitude to the inferior material realm, which actualizes as a consequence of Sophia's propensity for becoming or flux. The Valentinian πληρωμα is therefore dialectical in that there is both a potential and actual tension that characterizes its constitutional makeup. The divine (according to the Valentinian *Weltanschauung*) is both feminine and masculine: there are two cosmic principles in the πληρωμα (the fullness of divinity). One metaphysical substrate (the Father) experiences transcendent plenitude in an absolute sense. The other metaphysical principle (i.e. *Sophia*) is marginal and exceedingly prone to sin. Hence, Valentinus' concept of divine fullness is structurally dualistic, perhaps "patriarchal," yet theoretically differs from Plato's transcendent realm of Ideas since the eternal and supposedly immutable world of Valentinianism assumes or sublates (*aufheben*) the temporal and inferior realm of becoming, whereas Plato's intelligible realm of being remains manifestly distinct from the sensible realm that is characterized by Heraclitean flux (*panta rhei*). It never sublates it.[26]

The unintended philosophical consequence of this Valentinian theory is that both the sensible world and its Creator (δημιυργος) are inherently malignant; evil (that which causes pain, suffering or injury) originates with the godhead instead of stemming from humankind. Consequently, one must ask how successful the Gnostic explanation of evil really is since it links the source of pain, suffering and calamity with both intra and extra-pleromatic superhuman entities.

In conclusion, we can confidently state that Valentinian Christology resembles what we find in the Gospel of Truth (*Evangelium Veritatis*) in some respects. For instance, Valentinus posits a καταβασις for Christ the Redeemer who descends from on high and unites with Jesus, a hypostatic or personal entity that appears to be human, but is in essence wholly spiritual: "Thus for these Gnostics Jesus only seemed to be human. His entire earthly existence was a charade in which he pretended to be flesh and blood for his disciples' sake."[27] It is no wonder the Valentinians maintained that when Jesus of Nazareth met with death on the *crux*, the Gnostic Christ raised His mortal body or corpse *(mors mortis)* and transported it to the spiritual realms above (των ανω). In this manner, the Christ of Gnosticism prepared the way for others to enter the divine *pleroma*. Accordingly, he functioned as a forerunner (πρόδρομος) in behalf of the "elect."[28] This type of Christology seems to manifestly devalue the human body, however (Col 2:23). It is no wonder that certain phenomenologists of religion have described Gnosticism as "exilic" or anti-worldly.[29] The pessimistic tendencies and apparent heretical nature of the Gnostic schools undeniably accounted for the orthodox rejoinder to this patently syncretistic movement.

C. THE ORTHODOX RESPONSE TO GNOSTICISM

Gnosticism constituted a formidable challenge to the Christian faith. It was an acute religious threat that could easily have distorted (beyond recognition) the distinctive character and core essence of what many considered historical orthodox Christianity. However one defines the term "Christianity," *una voce*, believers of all stripes can no doubt agree with what Paul Tillich observes regarding Gnosticism: "If Christian theology had succumbed to this [Gnostic] temptation, the particular character of Christianity would have been lost. Its unique basis in the person of Jesus would have become meaningless."[30] But orthodox Christian theologians offered a successful riposte to the Gnostic challenge. These anti-Gnostic polemicists "fought against gnosticism [sic] and expelled it from the church."[31] In this way, the *regula fidei*, which the apostles supposedly transmitted to their successors, was purportedly preserved.

The three great anti-Gnostic theologians are Irenaeus, Tertullian, and Hippolytus.[32] Irenaeus (130–200 CE) stands out as the pre-eminent Christian polemicist, who opposed the divergent Gnostic schools of thought. He was a Greek speaker from Asia Minor, became bishop of Lyons, learned about Christianity from Polycarp of Smyrna (a student of the apostle John)[33] and possessed an in-depth knowledge of Scripture, having the ability "to systematize ideas and sum up an argument in a few pungent sentences."[34] Moreover, Irenaeus was evidently the pre-eminent anti-Gnostic theologian since he not only waged spiritual warfare against the Gnostics, but he also seemingly understood—to a great degree—the vital significance of Pauline theology for the Christian assembly.[35] Most notable among Irenaeus' achievements, however, is his inimitable and significant work, *Adversus Haereses* (*The Unmasking and Refutation of Falsely So-Called Gnosis*). The bishop of Lyons penned this treatise ca. 185 CE.[36] It is both a constructive and deconstructive treatise in that it simultaneously elucidates and decenters Gnostic theosophy.

Irenaeus' momentous theological composition consists of five books that counter Gnostic religious claims by placing the stress on episcopal, traditional, and canonical data.[37] Contra the Gnostics, Irenaeus avidly resists speculative notions regarding the inner life of the Godhead.[38] His tome also robustly opposes the inherent Docetism and patent dualism of being the Gnostic movement propagated.[39] Yet, Irenaeus not only decenters the Gnostic system,[40] but he spends time clarifying Christian *dogmata*, unambiguously setting out pragmatic theological principles that supposedly function as established control beliefs for orthodoxy.[41] Accordingly, Brunner sums up the theological contributions of Irenaeus as follows: "So the enterprise of theological dogmatics begins with a work which, in its very title, suggests its polemic and apologetic aim, the *Elenchus* of Irenaeus. The first great work of Christian theology is a controversial work against Gnosticism."[42] Another anti-Gnostic, one who also manifested schismatic tendencies, namely, Hippolytus, faithfully sustained the eristic project of Irenaeus.

1. Hippolytus

Hippolytus (ca. 160–236 CE) wrote a document entitled *Refutatio omnium haeresium* (*Refutation of All Heresies*). Scholars have also given it the appellative Φιλοσοφυμενα (*Philosophical Teachings*) based on the content of the first book contained in the work.[43] Hippolytus' Φιλοσοφυμενα actually is composed of two parts: books (*capita*) one and four as well as a subsequent section detailing various and sundry aspects of the Gnostic system (books five through ten).

Hippolytus borrows concepts from Irenaeus' *Adversus Haereses* but expands upon the arguments contained therein.[44] He believes that the Logos fully becomes Son only when He assumes humanity. For instance, the polemicist writes: "Now what Son of His own has God sent down through the flesh if not the Word, whom He addressed as Son in view of the fact that he was going to become such in future?"[45] He thus incorporates *Logov* theology to demonstrate the patent errors of Gnosticism and other putative heresies. Hippolytus exposes the seemingly problematic nature of Docetism while concomitantly affirming the authentic humanity of the Logos *ensarkos*. The Docetae, he avers, perpetuate both error and heresy when they argue for the quasi humanity of Jesus Christ.[46] Moreover, Hippolytus contends that human representatives of God actually beheld the Christ of history (the Logov enfleshed): they touched, saw, witnessed and heard the man that God made lower than the angels.[47] Understandably, Hippolytus is determined to uphold this basic tenet of orthodox Christianity. The full expression of the anti-Gnostic theologian's Logos theory, however, is ultimately actualized in Tertullian's treatises. We thus now turn our attention to this tireless fighter of ecclesiastical heresy.

2. Tertullian

Since we will evaluate Tertullian's exegesis of Ps 8:5 and discuss his heresiological activities below, this section will only offer a brief encapsulation of his passionate opposition to Gnosticism which is highlighted in *Adversus Valentianos* (*Against the Valentinians*).

Tertullian portrays the Valentinian Gnostics as distorters of truth: they are nothing but mythmakers, who officiously guard their sacred doctrine, in order to conceal their objective guilt before God and men: "The officiousness with which they guard their doctrine is an officiousness which betrays their guilt."[48] In a manner befitting the Eleusinian perpetuators of hallowed mysteries,[49] the Valentinians made silence, secrecy and esotericism, cardinal virtues: "In like manner, the heretics who are now the object of our remarks, the Valentinians, have formed Eleusinian dissipations of their own, consecrated by a profound silence, having nothing of the heavenly in them but their mystery."[50] Tertullian thus writes that the Valentinian Gnostics were intractable elitists who preserved their sacrosanct mysteries at all costs:

> If you intimate to them that you understand their opinions, they insist on knowing nothing themselves. If you come to a close engagement with them they destroy your own fond hope of a victory over them by a self-immolation. Not even to their own disciples do they commit a secret before they have made sure of them. They have the knack of persuading men before instructing them; although truth persuades by teaching, but does not teach by first persuading.[51]

Even more objectionable than their privileged esotericism, however, was the Christological Docetism that the Valentinians espoused. Docetism is the doctrine that maintains Christ was not fully human: He only appeared to be a flesh and blood man so that other human beings might see and touch Him or witness His "phantasmal" death. Tertullian's aversion to Valentinianism probably explains his intense dislike of Angelomorphic Christology.[52] Even so, as we have contended throughout this study, there are Angelomorphic elements implicitly and explicitly contained in his writings.

Having provided a historical context for Tertullian's Christology and his exegesis of Ps 8:5, we will now examine how the pre-Nicenes interpret this key passage in order to illuminate Tertullian's exegesis of the eighth psalm in *Adversus Praxean*. First, we will introduce the problemata associated with interpreting this verse. Subsequent to a look at the common problematic aspects related to this passage, we will review the pre-Nicene exegesis of Ps 8:5.

3. Problemata Associated with Psalm 8:5

One method that this study will utilize to support the contentions put forth herein is to make an appeal to the ante-Nicene exegesis of the eighth psalm. Each occurrence of Ps 8:5 listed in *Biblia Patristica* has been researched, analyzed and reflected upon in order that the patristic interpretation of the text can be fairly and contextually interpreted. The aforementioned examination has shown that there seems to be an interesting phenomenon in writers such as Tatian or Clement of Alexandria since neither theologian believes that Christ is the referential subject of the psalmist's song of praise to God. Tertullian, however, consistently applies Ps 8:5 to Christ, but he refers it to him in three different respects. We will deal with these instances below when reviewing the pre-Nicene exegesis of Ps 8:5.

Among other places, we encounter this OT verse in *Adversus Praxean* 9 where Tertullian writes, "He was made a little less on this side of the angels."[53] Before pointing to other occurrences of this text, however, there are certain problemata associated with this passage that we need to mention in passing. These interpretational difficulties need not detain us long. For while the Hebrew of Ps 8:5 is somewhat ambiguous and occasions no little controversy among Semitic scholars, the meaning of the psalm is transparent enough in Tertullian's treatises.

Peter Craigie contends that the translation "God" for the Hebrew *elohim* in Ps 8:5 "is almost certainly correct" and probably alludes to the image of God in humankind.[54] However, it is important to note that the LXX, Syriac OT, Vulgate and the Targumim all indicate that *elohim* in Ps 8:5 signifies "angels."[55] The pre-Nicenes also prefer the linguistic formula "angels" over against the translation "God" for Ps 8:5. Tertullian, Clement of Alexandria and Tatian conceive of the *elohim* or $\alpha\gamma\gamma\epsilon\lambda οι$ as "angels." Undoubtedly, they were influenced by the LXX or the NT account found in Heb 2:7.

D. EXEGESIS OF PS 8:5 BY THE GREEK AND LATIN PRE-NICENES

1. Tatian

Tatian (120–173 CE)[56] exegetes Ps 8:5 in a hortatory treatise addressed to the Greeks thus:[57]

> Of their own free will they [the demons] have handed down the laws of death to men, but after their loss of immortality men have overcome death by death in faith, and through repentance they have been given a calling, according to the

saying: 'since they were made for a little while lower than the angels'. It is possible for everyone defeated to win another time, if he rejects the constitution making for death; what this is can easily be seen by those who wish for immortality.[58]

The rhetorically oriented Assyrian explains that the angels who ceased glorifying God and subsequently became witting agents of the Devil possess free will. Nevertheless, these unholy, unsanctified spirits have utilized their God-given freedom of volition to hand down morbidity-inducing statutes that severely enslave or restrict humankind. Although humanity has lost the divine gift of immortality, Tatian does not believe that mortals are hopelessly condemned to lives of progressive mortification. The apologist declares that men "have overcome death by death in faith" even though they were "made for a little while lower than the angels." To whom is Tatian applying Ps 8:5? It appears that he applies the passage to "men" or humans. How, though, did God make humans temporarily lower than the angels, according to Tatian?

Tatian believes that humankind forfeited the potential for deathlessness in the Edenic Fall. Nevertheless, he is convinced that humans have the ability to regain "ultimate immortality" or deathlessness through the salvific activity of the Λογος.[59] Hence, he rejects the inherent immortality of the soul doctrine espoused by Greek philosophers such as Plato and Socrates. Moreover, the Stoic doctrine of inherent psychical deathlessness does not seem to fare any better in Tatian's hortatory address to the Greeks. There is no such thing as cyclical time for the rhetorical Assyrian. Life, for this early church writer, ultimately forms an "arc" of existence.[60] The arc (a geometrical metaphor invoked by Pelikan) represents the boundaries of human existence.[61]

Tatian declares that a terrestrial finite moral existent or creaturely essence does not possess an inherent rational or immortal soul, contra the Stoics. Nevertheless, bounded moral existents do differ from the beasts in that they are made in God's image:

> Man is not, as the croakers teach, a rational being capable of intelligence and understanding (for according to them even the irrational creatures will be proved capable of intelligence and understanding), but man alone is "the image and the likeness of God." I mean by man not one who behaves like the animals, but one who has advanced far beyond his humanity towards God himself.[62]

The Assyrian *rhetor* does not associate the image of God with an imperishable or rational soul.[63] Rather, one witnesses the *imago dei* actualized in humanity when a representative finite moral existent advances: "far beyond his humanity toward God himself," evidently making God the *summum bonum* or telov of his life. Immortality is consequently worthless if one possesses an existence incapable of experiencing *qanatov*, but is eternally or everlastingly separated from God. Fortunately, humans can overcome death by submitting to death in faith, that is, by offering themselves to God as martyrs, Tatian thinks.[64] Most importantly, Christ submitted to a death in faith so that other men and women could be set free from enslavement to demonically originated mortality:

> But matter desired to exercise lordship over the soul; and according to their freewill these gave laws of death to men; but men, after the loss of immortality, have conquered death by submitting to death in faith; and by repentance a call has been given to them, according to the word which says, "Since they were made a little lower than the angels." And, for every one who has been conquered, it is possible again to conquer, if he rejects the condition which brings death.

It is evident that Tatian applies Ps 8:5 to redeemed humans and does not interpret it as a reference to Christ. He is not alone in this regard.

2. Clement of Alexandria

Clement of Alexandria (d. 215 CE) believed that Ps 8:5 is a hymnic prophecy foretelling the pistic activity of learned, advanced or mature Christians: the ones whom Clement labels "true Gnostics."[65] He declares:

> And what, I ask, is it in which man differs from beasts, and the angels of God, on the other hand, are wiser than he? "Thou madest him a little lower than the angels." For some do not interpret this Scripture of the Lord, although He also bore flesh, but of the perfect man and the gnostic, inferior in comparison with the angels in time, and by reason of the vesture [of the body]. I call then wisdom nothing but science, since life differs not from life.[66]

Clement suggests that humankind is set apart from the beasts and angels in that God elevated humanity above the animals when he created man and woman but made women and men "lower than the angels." Clement's application of Ps 8:5 is more precise, however. In particular, he reports that certain Christians of his time, whom he does not name or identify, did not regard the psalm as a reference to the Messiah, although they believed that Christ became flesh and resided with humans for a time. Instead, these "anonymous Christians" thought that Ps 8:5 refers to "the perfect man and the Gnostic." Clement is undoubtedly being quite subtle here. He himself was one such Christian, who thought the Lord Jesus Christ did not fulfill the passage about humans becoming lower than the angels; his clever mention of "some" Christians thus is not wholly unexpected.

The Gnostic Christian (i.e. advanced or mature intellectual believer), Clement explains, is inferior (lower) than spirit beings are vis-à-vis the angels' relation to time and "by reason of the vesture [of the body]."⁶⁷ Hence, Clement appears to say that some of his Christian contemporaries believed that followers of Jesus Christ in the here-and-now are lower than the angels, but will not be inferior to holy spiritual essences after the divestiture of the imperfect body that poignantly burdens authentic "Gnostic" followers of Christ in this age. Clement's further comments in his work *Stromata* (*Miscellanies*) support this understanding of the Clementine text:

> Accordingly it is said, "God talked with Moses as a friend with a friend." That, then, which is true being clear to God, forthwith generates truth. And the Gnostic loves the truth. "Go," it is said, "to the ant, thou sluggard, and be the disciple of the bee;" thus speaks Solomon. For if there is one function belonging to the peculiar nature of each creature, alike of the ox, and horse, and dog, what shall we say is the peculiar function of man? He is like, it appears to me, the Centaur, a Thessalian figment, compounded of a rational and irrational part, of soul and body. Well, the body tills the ground, and hastes to it; but the soul is raised to God: trained in the true philosophy, it speeds to its kindred above, turning away from the lusts of the body, and besides these, from toil and fear, although we have shown that patience and fear belong to the good man.⁶⁸

True to his Neo-Platonic orientation, Clement conceives the veritable Gnostic in dualistic terms. The authentic Gnostic is a compound of rationality and irrationality, of soul and body, spirit and flesh. The body is inferior to the soul. It is a requisite temporal medium permitting Christians to exist in the here-and-now. Nonetheless, Clement believes that the temporal and provisional corpus belonging to humankind hastens to the ground, eventually returning to the dust. Conversely, the Alexandrian thinker argues that God elevates the soul trained in "true philosophy" to the very heavens of God's presence. The soul of the true Gnostic consequently advances to its eternal, actual and abiding home, finally liberated from lust, toil and fear. The advanced Christian believer, in imitation of God (as Clement and the pre-Nicenes generally envisage Him), masters the divine quality of $\alpha\pi\alpha\theta\epsilon\iota\alpha$ before death.⁶⁹ The precocious Christian is only lower than the angels while subsisting in the flesh. However, God crowns genuine Gnostics with interminable and peerless honor and glory, eventually exalting such disciples of Christ above the angels.

E. TERTULLIAN'S EXEGETICAL APPROACH TO PS 8:5

Tertullian may have been familiar with how Clement of Alexandria and Tatian exegeted Ps 8:5. Furthermore, he probably knew that not all Christians viewed the text as a prophecy regarding the Lord Jesus Christ. Yet, Tertullian consistently applied the text messianically (in three diverse ways). We will now examine his respective construals of Ps 8:5 in order to set the stage for how he conscripts the passage in *Adversus Praxean*.

First, Tertullian associates the saying in Ps 8:5 concerning the minoration of the Son with the protological intermediate agent through whom the Father produced the cosmos. He writes:

> For we claim also that Christ has always acted in God the Father's name, has Himself ever since the beginning associated with, and conversed with, patriarchs and prophets. He is the Son of the Creator, His Word whom by bringing Him forth from Himself He caused to be His Son. From then onwards He put Him in authority over his whole design and purpose, reducing Him a little below the angels, as it is written in David. By this reduction He was brought by the Father to these <acts and experiences> which you disapprove of as human: for He was learning even from the beginning, by so early assuming manhood, to be that which He was going to be at the end.[70]

Tertullian, reminiscent of Lactantius, believes that Christ[71] has functioned as the Father's representative (*in dei patris nomine*) since the beginning of God's creation.[72] As the expressed Logos (λογος προφορικος) begotten before and for the purpose of creation, the pre-incarnate being who became flesh in the first century of our common era discoursed with the ancient Hebrew "patriarchs and prophets" and in this capacity fulfilled His exalted role as the *sermo* or *ratio dei*. Tertullian repeats a familiar theme in a passage culled from his treatise against Hermogenes. He reiterates the fact that God caused His own Word "to be His Son." There was thus a time when God did not have a Son as such (*Adv Herm* 3.18), according to the ancient Carthaginian.

Before His temporal generation, Tertullian contends that the Son was Wisdom, Word and *ratio dei*. That is, the North African apologist thinks that the one who became Christ was more than likely an impersonal divine attribute (divine immanent thought) or at least, not fully personal per His *actus essendi*.[73] Subsequent to the *nativitas perfecta sermonis*,[74] however, Tertullian explains that God the Father placed the entity that eventually became His Son "in authority over His whole design and purpose" (*exinde omni dispositioni suae voluntatique praefecit*): the Father appointed Christ as the protological mediator of creation.[75] Nonetheless, by proceeding forth as the pre-eminent Son of God before and for creation, the LogoV became lower than angels, so that He might both govern creation and reveal Himself to the ancient patriarchs and prophets in order to provide a foregleam of the enfleshment that would function as the divine basis for reconciling humankind to God (2 Cor 5:18–20) in the first century CE.[76] In addition, this minoration of the Son, His becoming lower than the angels as the pre-existent Son *qua* Son, also made it possible for Christ to learn through social intercourse with humans, how to be a human being.

1. Tertullian's Exegesis of Psalm 8:5 and the Angelophanic Son

Tertullian not only assigns Ps 8:5 to the pre-existent Son of God; he further applies this verse to the angelophanic Son. Specifically, Tertullian believes that another way in which the Logos became lower than the angels was by entering into discourse with humankind via visions, dreams, or other forms of supernatural phenomena. Tertullian explains this form of filial minoration in *Adv Prax* 16. We will offer an analysis of this *caput* in the study's final chapter. For now, it is sufficient to note that Tertullian identified the one who conversed with Adam, the patriarchs and prophets as God's Son in the capacity of *malak YHWH*. By manifesting Himself as an angel to the patriarchs and prophets, Christ demonstrated his minor status in relation to celestial creaturely essences, Tertullian argues. The angelophanies recorded in the OT were adumbrations of Christ's first century earthly manifestation: "By this reduction He was brought by the Father to these <acts and experiences> which you [Marcion] disapprove of as human: for He was learning even from the beginning, by so early assuming manhood, to be that which He was going to be at the end."[77] Yet, there is another way in which the apologist applies the text to the Son.

2. Tertullian's Exegesis of Psalm 8:5 in Relation to the Incarnate Son

Tertullian's third application of Ps 8:5 pertains to the incarnate or enfleshed Son of God. In fact, he predominantly refers this passage to the Logos become human, who for a time came to be lower than angels. We will now consider how Tertullian utilizes this passage when discussing the Son in His humanity.

We have already observed Tertullian insisting that the Son is an angel "by a term of office" and not as nature (*ut natura*). After all, he writes: *dictus est quidem magni consilii angelus, id est nuntius, officii non naturae vocabulo*.[78] The Son is thus an angel in that "He was to announce to the world the Father's great project, that [plan] concerned with the restitution of man" (*magnum enim cogitatem patris, super hominis scilicet restitutionem, adnuntiaturus saeculo erat*).[79] Conversely, Tertullian reasons that the Son must not be reckoned with the angels ontologically because he functions as an angel in God's *dispositio* or *oikonomia*. Nevertheless, he employs the designation *angelus* with reference to the Son in order that he might refute the doctrine of Ebion: It is at this point that the *rhetor* again invokes Ps 8:5, applying it to the Logos *ensarkos*:

> So I shall find it easier to say, if I have to, that the Son Himself was the angel (that is, the messenger) of the Father, than that there was an angel in the Son. But seeing that the Son Himself is the subject of the pronouncement, Thou hast made Him a little lower than the angels, how shall He be thought to have clothed Himself with an angel when He is made lower than the angels by being made man (as being flesh and soul) and the Son of Man? For as the Spirit of God, and the Power of the Most High, He cannot be held to be lower than the angels, seeing He is God, and the Son of God. So then, even as he is made less than the angels while clothed with manhood, even so He is not less if clothed with an angel.[80]

The Ebionites contended that an angel took the place of Christ's human soul when He became flesh. To combat this concept, Tertullian maintains that "as Spirit of God, and the Power of the Most High," Christ is not lower than the angels.[81] This perplexing statement implies that Tertullian, at this stage in his career and even possibly later, adhered to a form of binitarianism and was not a Trinitarian as such. The apologist maintains that the entity known as the Spirit and Power of God, which became the Son of God, was not at the outset functionally or ontologically subordinate to the angels. But Tertullian's statement becomes a little perplexing when we detect him paralleling Spirit of God and Power of the Most High with God and Son of God, especially since he applies the latter terms to the Son.[82]

Tertullian is evidently less than precise here since he elsewhere makes marked distinctions between the Son *qua* Son and the Logos as God's *Ratio*. Furthermore, he explicitly declares that the Son as such has been lower than the angels ever since He became God's *filius*. Hence, Tertullian can hardly mean that the Christ in his capacity as Son (enfleshed or pre-enfleshed) is not inferior to the angels.

Finally, Tertullian also cites Ps 8:5 when attempting to refute the Valentinians and Jews. The next quotation illustrates how he utilizes this Biblical passage apologetically:

> They find it written, Thou hast made him a little less than the angels, yet they deny the inferior substance of Christ, though he declares himself not even a man but a worm, though he had no form nor comeliness, but his aspect was ignoble, worn out more than all men, and he was a man under chastisement, and knowing how to bear weaknesses. They acknowledge a man, mingled with God, yet deny the manhood: they believe he died, yet that which died they claim was born of incorruption—as though corruption were anything else but death . . . Have

patience. Christ has not yet put down all his enemies, so as to triumph over his enemies, with his friends to share his victory.[83]

In total contradistinction to the Valentinians, Tertullian affirms the complete humanity, that is, the "inferior substance (*inferiorem substantiam*) of Jesus Christ."[84] No doubt, the apologist has in mind the biblical Psalm, which proclaims that God's Messiah was not even a man. Rather, he was a lowly despicable worm in the estimation of those who doubted His God-given authority: "But I am a worm, not a man; the scorn of men, despised by the people" (Ps 22:7 NAB).[85] Nevertheless, the Son was made lower than the angels for a time that God might later crown Him with unparalleled glory and honor. The fact that the Psalmist indicates Christ would be subordinate to the angels while enfleshed is evidence of His genuine manhood for Tertullian and provides an irrefutable rejoinder to Docetic claims.

This analysis of the pre-Nicene exegesis of Ps 8:5 demonstrates that while not all ancient Christian exegetes thought the passage referred to the katabatic activity of the Messiah or the minoration of the Son, Tertullian consistently employed the text to refute what he thought were unorthodox Christological formulations. Tertullian utilized the verse to establish the true humanity of Jesus Christ. He further spoke of the Son becoming lower than the angels when He as the *malak YHWH* appeared to ancient Hebrew patriarchs and prophets such as Abraham and Jacob. Most important for our purposes, however, it is clear that Tertullian believes God made the pre-incarnate Son inferior to the angels when He uttered the generative words, *fiat lux* (*Adv Marc* 2:27). We will return to this point in the final portion of the study.

Excursus: Ebionites

Ebion (ca. 175 CE) allegedly believed that Jesus was an ordinary man (*nudum hominem*) of King David's lineage. According to this distinctive form of so-called Jewish Christianity, Jesus of Nazareth was a descendant of David, Solmon's father. He was not, however, "the Son of God" (*et tantum ex semine David, id est non et dei filium*).[86] The Ebionites were adoptionists, affirming neither the pre-existence nor the Virgin Birth of the Son.[87] Jesus was simply a "normal human" (ψιλος ανθρωπος) whose generation was unnatural or unspectacular: He was a creature that God highly exalted when a heavenly angelic being became one with Jesus of Nazareth at His baptism.[88] The righteousness of Christ is what distinguished Jesus from other humans as did His God-given vocation.[89]

On the other hand, at least one form of Ebionitism taught that Jesus was more illustrious than the OT prophets were since an angel spoke through Him. Nevertheless, Tertullian offers the following retort to this type of adoptionist Christology: "For he was himself the Lord, declaring openly and on his own authority, But I say unto you" (*ipse enim erat dominus, coram et ex sua auctoritate pronuntians, Ego autem dico vobis*).[90]

Tertullian states that there was no need for Jesus to speak through an angel. He was God's messenger (*angelus*) sent to effect reconciliation between God and humanity. He could therefore speak on the basis of His own authority. There is also a sense, Tertullian writes, in which the Son is God. Whether he believed that the Son is fully God (*vere deus*), however, remains to be seen.

In any event, the Ebionites apparently received their designation from those who opposed the Jewish Christian movement. The appellation given to the group may denote "those who are poor," although we cannot be indubitably certain of the etymology behind the seemingly descriptive title.[91] Grillmeier supplies four reasons why opponents of certain Jewish-Christian adoptionists labeled them Ebionites. He attributes it to the purportedly scant intelligence of the Ebionites, the destitute state of the law they followed, their impoverished estimation of Christ, and their meager comprehension of hope and works.[92] But even Grillmeier recognizes that certain antagonistic claims concerning Ebionite Jesuology were evidently mistaken since the Ebionite doctrine of the "marginal Jew" from Nazareth clearly had a transcendent dimension that went beyond viewing him as a mere man.[93] Furthermore, these Jewish Christians were not monolithic but heterogeneous in nature.[94] Regardless of their authentic adoptionists beliefs, Tertullian countered their Christological claims by appealing to Ps 8:5.

NOTES

1. Maria L. Colish, *The Stoic Tradition from Antiquity to the Early Middle Ages*, 2 vol. (Leiden: Brill, 1985), 2:12.

2. Pokorny is no doubt correct when he observes that the evidence for a first century form of Gnosticism is not "unequivocally attested." But we can surmise that an incipient form of Gnosticism probably obtained in the first century in view of the data contained in John's Gospel and the Pauline Epistles. See Petr Pokorny, *Colossians: A Commentary* (Peabody: Hendrickson, 1991), 117.

3. See Stanley M. Burgess, *The Holy Spirit: Ancient Christian Traditions* (Peabody: Hendrickson, 1984), 35; Paul Tillich, *A History of Christian Thought* (New York: Harper and Row, 1968), 33. Kelly is hesitant to call Gnosticism a movement. He considers the term "misleading" when applied to the Gnostic religion since the terminology seems to imply that Gnosticism was a "concrete organization or church." Even he has to concede, however, that the systems or schools labeled Gnosticism have enough in common to be categorized in some form or fashion. This study therefore takes the position that the syncretistic religio-philosophical phenomenon known as Gnosticism qualifies as a movement in a sociological sense. See J. N. D. Kelly, *Early*

Christian Doctrines (San Francisco: Harper and Row, 1978), 25. Studer reasons that the various schools and sects of Gnosticism are so homogeneous that it is not "unreasonable" to regard the philosophical-religious phenomenon as a "movement" (*Trinity and Incarnation*, 55).

4. Olson prefers the terminology "schools" or "movements." He reports that Irenaeus studied twenty Gnostic schools of thought and set out their similarities and differences in detail. *Vide* Roger Olson, *The Story of Christian Theology: Twenty Centuries of Tradition and Reform* (Downers Grove: InterVarsity Press, 1999), 37ff.

5. Pokorny, *Colossians*, 117.

6. Burgess, *Holy Spirit*, 35.

7. Pelikan, *Christian Tradition*, 1:85

8. Ibid.

9. Ibid. Richard Melick also cites Lohse who contends that Valentianian Gnosticism teaches that God does not belong to the πληρωμα. See *Philippians, Colossians, and Philemon: An Exegetical and Theological Exposition of Holy Scripture*, NAC (Nashville: Broadman Press, 1991), 223.

10. Pelikan, Christian Tradition, 1:85.

11. Chadwick, *The Early Church*, 33–34.

12. Ibid. 35.

13. Theoreticians have traditionally formulated the problem of evil in terms of the logical and emotive or existential problem of evil. The Gnostics seemed to have concerned themselves with the question, "Unde malum?" Helpful discussions of the distinction between the logical and existential problem of evil can be found in Stephen T. Davis, *Logic and the Nature of God* (Grand Rapids: Eerdmans, 1983), 97–117; Alvin Plantinga, *God, Freedom, and Evil* (Grand Rapids: Eerdmans, 1974); Hal Flemings, *A Philosophical, Scientific and Theological Defense for the Notion that A God Exists* (Lanham: University Press of America, 2003). Tertullian alludes to the Valentinian interest in the question, "Whence comes evil?" See *De Prae Haer* 7.5.

14. Valentinus was evidently an intelligent and well-spoken individual. He claimed to have received a secret Christian tradition from Theudas, one of the apostle Paul's disciples. Consult E. Pagels, *The Gnostic Gospels* (New York: Random House, 1978), 36. Paul putatively only taught such esoteric wisdom (σοφια) to a select few disciples (ibid. 37).

15. Pagels, *Gnostic Gospels*, 39.

16. See Riemer Roukema, *Gnosis and Faith in Early Christianity* (London, SCM Press, 1999), 129.

17. Bruce M. Metzger, *The Canon of the New Testament* (Oxford: Clarendon Press, 1997), 81.

18. Roukema, *Gnosis and Faith*, 130.

19. See Frend, *Rise of Christianity*, 207; Olson, *Story of Theology*, 37.

20. Ialdabaoth is supposed to be the God that the Jews invoked by using the Tetragrammaton, the four consonants *YHWH*. *Vide* Frend, *Rise of Christianity*, 207.

21. Homer's *Iliad* contains myths that try to account for evil in a manner analogous to the Gnostics narratives. See Mark P. O. Morford and Robert J. Lenardon, *Classical Mythology* (New York: Longman, 1999), 370–371.

22. For a discussion of the distinction between "natural" and moral evil, see Plantinga, *God, Freedom and Evil* and Flemings, *A Philosophical, Scientific and Theological Defense*.

23. Hans Jonas, *The Gnostic Religion: The Message of the Alien God and the Beginnings of Christianity* (Boston: Bacon Press, 1963), 285.

24. See *Five Stages of Greek Religion* (Garden City: Doubleday, 1955), 154.

25. Chadwick, *The Early Church*, 35.

26. Ibid.

27. See *Republic* 505–511.

28. Olson, *The Story of Theology*, 38.

29. Robert M. Grant, *Gnosticism and Christianity* (New York: Harper and Row, 1966), 136ff. Metzger (*The Canon of the NT*, 81) demonstrates that the Gnostics categorized human beings into three groups, the πνεθματικοι (genuine or elect Gnostics), ψυκικοι (ordinary and unenlightened Christians), and the *f*likoi (those exclusively composed of matter and destined for eternal condemnation). See *Adv Haer* 1.6.1. Cf. S. Hall, *Doctrine and Practice in the Early Church* (Grand Rapids: Eerdmans, 1991), 43.

30. Merold Westphal, *God, Guilt and Death: An Existential Phenomenology of Religion* (Bloomington: Indiana University Press, 1987), 173–175.

31. Tillich, *A History of Christian Thought*, 36.

32. Ibid. 37.

33. Two other early theologians who offered powerful rejoinders to the contentions of Gnosticism are Clement of Alexandria (*Stromata* 3.4.30) and Origen (*Commentary on John*). Clement describes the Gnostics thus: "Talia etiam statuunt Prodici quoque asseclae, qui seipsos falso nomine vocant Gnosticos."

34. Harold O. J. Brown, *Heresies: Heresy and Orthodoxy in the History of the Church* (Peabody: Hendrickson, 1998), 78.

35. Frend, *Rise of Christianity*, 244.

36. Tillich, *A History of Christian Thought*, 37.

xxxvii Howard F. Vos, *Exploring Church History* (Nashville: Thomas Nelson, 1994), 17.

37. Ibid.

38. Brown, *Heresies*, 80.

39. Gnosticism influenced the dualism of Docetism. See Kurt Rudolph, *Gnosis: The Nature and History of an Ancient Religion*, trans. Robert M. Wilson (Edinburgh: T & T Clark, 1983), 372. Countering Docetism, Irenaeus writes: "Fasting forty days, like Moses and Elias, He afterwards hungered, first, in order that we may perceive that He was a real and substantial man — for it belongs to a man to suffer hunger when fasting; and secondly, that His opponent might have an opportunity of attacking Him" (*Adv Haer* 5.21.2).

40. Irenaeus castigates the numerological tendencies of the Gnostics, observing: "Moreover, they possess no proof of their system, which has but recently been invented by them, sometimes resting upon certain numbers, sometimes on syllables, and sometimes, again, on names; and there are occasions, too, when, by means of

those letters which are contained in letters, by parables not properly interpreted, or by certain [baseless] conjectures, they strive to establish that fabulous account which they have devised" (Ibid. 2.28.8).

41. Vos calls Irenaeus the "Father of Church Dogmatics" because of his constructive tendency vis-à-vis Christian theology (*Exploring*, 17).

42. Emil Brunner, *The Christian Doctrine of God*, vol. 1 of *Dogmatics*, trans. Olive Wyon (London: Lutterworth, 1949), 94. The term *elenchus* denotes a refutation or cross-examination.

43. Rudolph, *Gnosis*, 13.

44. Vos, *Exploring*, 17.

45. *Contra Noet* 15.6.

46. *Refutatio* 8:1–4.

47. The apostle John affirms the genuine humanity of Christ. He testifies in the opening passage of his First Epistle (NRSV): "We declare to you what was from the beginning, what we have heard, what we have seen with our eyes, what we have looked at and touched with our hands, concerning the word of life."

48. *Adv Val* 1. *Culpa*, like the English substantive "guilt," can refer to a sense of guilt (i.e. subjective culpability) or to an actual state of blameworthiness (objective guilt). Tertullian thought that the Valentinians were objectively guilty before God and men, but they tried to conceal it by means of their esoteric activities. They made an appeal to those who took pride in sacred mysteries. Subjective guilt may have led them to seek refuge in inscrutability.

49. See Moreford and Leonardon, *Classical Mythology*, 239–249.

50. *Adv Val* 1.

51. Ibid.

52. See Talbert, "Redeemer" 434; Carrell, *Jesus and the Angels*, 101.

53. Vg (Ps 8:6) reads: "Minuisti eum paulo minus ab angelis, gloria et honore coronasti eum." The writer of Hebrews, evidently quoting from the LXX, renders the psalm thus: ἄτων δε βραχύ τι παρ' αγγελους ἠλαττωμενον.

54. See *Psalms 1–50*, WBC (Waco: Word, 1983), 108.

55. Ibid.

56. Tatian was born in Assyria and eventually became a student of Justin Martyr. The *Oratio* is his best and most useful work, according to Eusebius. See *Oratio ad Graecos and Fragments*, trans. Molly Whittaker (Oxford: Clarendon Press, 1982), x. Tatian converted to Christianity as a result of a careful perusal of the "barbaric writings" (i.e. the Scriptures) of Judaism and Christianity. See *Oratio* 30. Later, he supposedly became an austere heretic, but we cannot conclusively substantiate the heretical nature of Tatian's teachings (Little, *Apologists*, 179–180). Whittaker thinks that it is hard to determine Tatian's orthodoxy or heretical status on the basis of the *Oratio* alone (*Oratio*, xvi). Tatian, while emphasizing gnwsiV in the manner of his famed heretical counterparts, the Gnostics, does not mention intermediary agents (aeons) who are part of some divine πληρωμα nor does he juxtapose the Most High (*altissimus*) with a mere demiurgical creator. See ibid., xvii. Tatian also received training as a rhetor. He eventually settled in Rome.

Chapter Two

57. *Oratio* 15.4–10.

58. ὁι δε ανθρωποι μετα την της αθανασιας αποβολην θανατω τω δια πιστεως τον θανατον νενικηκασιν και δια μετανοιας κλησις αυτοις δεδωρπται κατα τον ειποντα λογον επειδη βραχυ τι παρ' αγγελους ἠλαττωθσαν δυνατον δε παντι τω νενικημενω παλιν νικαν του θανατου την συστασιν παραιτουμενον τις δε εστιν ἁυτη ευσυνοπτον εσται τοις βουλομενοις ανθρωποις το αθανατον.

59. Jaroslav Pelikan, *The Shape of Death: Life, Death, and Immortality in the Early Fathers* (London: Macmillan, 1962), 18.

60. Ibid. 19.

61. Ibid. 22.

62. *Oratio* 15.10–16.

63. J. Pelikan, *The Shape of Death*, 22.

64. Ibid. 27

65. Burgess informs us that Clement "is concerned to distinguish the 'true gnostic' from the false gnostic or heretic. The true Gnostic is one who has indeed gained knowledge from God" (*Ancient Christian Traditions*, 71). Brown appears to be less sympathetic to Clement's seeming affinity for Gnostic terms. He implies that Clement may have been unduly influenced by heretical Gnostic concepts. See *Heresies*, 87. On the other hand, Bediako identifies the Clementine "Gnostic" as an "enlightened man" or "Christian scholar." See *Theology and Identity: The Impact of Culture upon Christian Thought in the Second Century and in Modern Africa* (Oxford: Regnum Books, 1992), 187.

66. *Stromata* 4.8.7.

67. Ibid.

68. Ibid.

69. Απαθεια in this context basically has reference to the inward quality of immunity to disturbance or perturbation. It refers to a state of impassibility, which supposedly characterizes the God of Christians. See Pelikan, *The Christian Tradition*, 1:52–53.

70. *Adv Marc* 2.27: "Nam et profitemur Christum semper egisse in dei patris nomine, ipsum ab initio conversatum, ipsum congressum cum patriarchis et prophetis, filium creatoris, sermonem eius, quem ex semetipso proferendo filium fecit, et exinde omni dispositioni suae voluntatique praefecit, diminuens illum modico citra angelos, sicut apud David scriptum est; qua diminutione in haec quoque dispositus est a patre quae ut humana reprehenditis, ediscens iam inde a primordio, iam inde homniem <indutus, id esse> quod erat futurus in fine."

71. Tertullian argues that the title Christ is a name given to the Son during God's reconciliatory dispensation or economy: "The name of Christ, however, does not arise from nature, but from dispensation; and so becomes the proper name of Him to whom it accrues in consequence of the dispensation" (*Adv Marc* 3.15).

72. See Lactantius, *Institutes* 4.14. Origen also calls the pre-existent Christ, God's "minister" in the preface of *De Prin*.

73. O'Collins perceptively notes: "Tertullian appears to have held that the divine Word, after existing within the Father's mind, then became a distinct person in a

'complete birth (*nativitas perfecta*) . . . only when creation began." See *The Tripersonal God*, 108.

74. *Adv Prax* 7.3.
75. *Adv Marc* 2.27.
76. Compare *De Carne* 6.
77. *Adv Marc* 2.27.
78. See *De Carne* 14.17–32.
79. Ibid, 14.17.
80. Ibid. 14.17–32: "magnum enim cogitatem patris, super hominis scilicet restitutionem, adnuntiaturus saeculo erat. Non ideo tamen sic angelus intellegendus ut aliqui Gabriel aut Michael. Nam et filius a domino vineae mittitur ad vinitores, sicut et famuli, de fructibus petitum: sed non propterea unus ex famulis deputabitur filius quia famulorum successit officio. facilius ergo dicam, si forte, ipsum filium angelum (id est nuntium) patris, quam angelum in filio. sed cum de [filio] ipso sit pronuntiatum, Minuisti eum modicum quid citra angelos deminutus dum homo fit, qua caro et anima, et filius hominis? Qua autem spiritus dei et virtus altissimi non potest infra angelos haberi, deus scilicet et dei filius. Quanto ergo, dum hominem gestat, minor angelis factus est, tanto non, dum angelum gestat."
81. *De Carne* 14.29–30.
82. Ibid.
83. *De Carne* 15.29–38: "Legunt denique, Minorasti eum modico citra angelos, et negant inferiorem substantiam Christi nec hominem se sed vernem pronuntiantis, qui nec formam habuit nec speciem, sed forma eius ignobilis, defecta citra omnes homines, homo in plaga et sciens ferre imbecillitatem. Agnoscunt hominem deo mixtum, et negant hominem: mortuum credunt, et quod est mortuum ex incorruptela natum esse contendunt, quasi corruptela aliud sit a morte. 'Sed et nostra caro statim resurgere debebat.' Exspecta: nondum inimicos suos Christus oppressit, ut cum amicis de inimicis triumphet."
84. Ibid.
85. Compare the "suffering servant" of *YHWH* motif in Isa 53.
86. *De Carne* 14.32–33.
87. See Ehrman, *The Orthodox Corruption*, 51; Carrell, *Jesus and the Angels*, 102; Studer, *Trinity and Incarnation*, 35–36.
88. Grillmeier, *Christ in Christian Tradition*, 92.
89. Ehrman, *The Orthodox Corruption*, 51. For information on the *Epistula Apostolorum* (a second century CE document possibly of Egyptian provenance) which "envisages Christ appearing as Gabriel," according to Carrell, *Jesus and the Angels*, 103.
90. *De Carne* 14.38–39.
91. Daniélou writes that the Ebionite tag did not derive from the individual named Ebion (contra Epiphanius) but actually originated from the Hebrew word *ebyon* meaning "poor" (1:55–56). Both Irenaeus (*Adv Haer* 1.26.2) and Origen (*Contra Celsum* 2.1) also mention this so-called heretical group.
92. Grillmeier, *Christ in the Christian Tradition*, 90. For an opposing view, see Chadwick, *Early Church*, 23. He briefly argues that the Ebionites were not given the

appellation by their enemies. Nor were they associated with the legendary figure named Ebion.

93. Grillmeier, *Christ in the Christian Tradition*, 91.

94. Ehrman accordingly disputes Daniélou's account since the latter depicts the Ebionites as a clearly demarcated movement in the ancient period. See *The Orthodox Corruption*, 56.

Chapter Three

Formal Introduction to *Adversus Praxean*

The identity of the purported heretic, Praxeas, has often proved to be elusive for historians of Christian dogma. Exactly who was the religious figure that managed to provoke Tertullian's ire? What did he teach? Why did the Latin writer from Carthage fervently oppose Praxeas' particular form of Christian teaching (διδαχη)? We will now address these three questions while formally examining *capita* one and two of *Adversus Praxean*.

A. THE IDENTITY OF PRAXEAS

The only ancient heresiologists to mention Praxeas are pseudo-Tertullian,[1] Augustine and Gennadius.[2] Some scholars consequently think that Tertullian invented the name *Praxeas* to protect the identity of bishop Zephyrinus (199–217) or his mysterious successor Callistus (217–22).[3] Nevertheless, one problem with this identification is that none of the extant data suggests that either cleric came from Asia, as Tertullian seems to say about his rival.[4] Furthermore, the theological beliefs of Zephyrinus and Callistus are less than certain, based on the extant data. On the other hand, the fact that neither bishop hailed from Asia may not be an impediment to viewing one of these individuals as the real Praxeas since Tertullian does not actually state that his antagonist personally hailed from Asia: it was only his aberrant Christological doctrine that emanated from that place.[5]

While the exact referential significance of Praxeas remains unknown,[6] with some degree of certainty we can contend that Praxeas apparently taught that the Father and Son are hypostatically identical (*duos unum volunt esse, ut idem pater et filius habeatur*).[7] Moreover, he simultaneously propagated the notion that the Father co-suffered with the Son since the second Person of the Trinity was supposed to be the man Jesus of Nazareth, whereas Praxeas identified Christ (the divine in Jesus) with the Father.[8] In other words, the enigmatic rival of Tertullian taught a form of Modalistic Monarchianism: the belief that the Father, Son and Holy Spirit are three self-identical and successive divine modes of being.[9] Does the historical record indicate that Zephryinus or Callistus were modalists, however?

Frend cites Hippolytus who describes Zephyrinus as "an uneducated simpleton."[10] This "unsophisticated" bishop may have believed that God and Jesus Christ constitute an undifferentiated metaphysical unity. Although he did not think that God (*in se*) is able to suffer and die as the Son did, Zephyrinus nonetheless had difficulty adequately distinguishing the *tres personae trinitatis*. Frend considers the works of Hippolytus and Pseudo-Tertullian independent testimony supporting the notion that bishop Victor, Zephyrinus or possibly Callistus inclined toward the theological views of Praxeas. Moreover, he reports that Modalism remained "deeply ingrained" in Roman Trinitarian thought long after the time of Tertullian.[11] Divine hypostatic oneness was most certainly the belief of the *simplices*, who evidently constituted the majority of believers in Rome. Fortman, however, maintains that the testimony found in Hippolytus' *Refutatio* (9.6–7) does not necessarily confirm that Zephryinus was a modalist or that he was "Praxeas." Besides statements that appear to contradict themselves in the *Refutatio*, "Hippolytus is such an impassioned and hostile witness that it is difficult to accept his testimony as the simple truth."[12]

Hippolytus considered Callistus a modalist as well. While Callistus purportedly distinguished between the Father and the Son by regarding the Father as the Spirit indwelling the Son and the Son as "the human body of Jesus,"[13] Hippolytus argued that the Roman bishop made no actual hypostatic distinction between the Father and Son. Nevertheless, the misgivings that Hippolytus had for Callistus must be taken into consideration.[14] Consequently, we must admit that reliable evidence for the identity of Praxeas remains unknown. Yet, why did Praxean theology provoke Tertullian's ire?

B. TERTULLIAN'S OPPOSITION TO PRAXEAN CHRISTOLOGY

Tertullian essentially portrays Praxeas as an unwitting pawn of the Devil: a demon-inspired instrument who manifestly (albeit unknowingly) opposes Christian truth in a variety of diabolic ways (*varie diabolus aemulatus est veritatem*).[15] One method that the Devil employs to oppose Christianity, writes Tertullian, is the *modus operandi* of pretending to defend Christian verity (*Varie diabolus aemulatus est veritatem. adfectavit illam aliquando defendendo concutere*) in order that he might ultimately subvert it.[16] The chief opponent of God (*ha Satan*) occasionally plays the part of a genuine theistic apologist, but Tertullian argues that even on those occasions he obfuscates passages in sacred Scripture, especially those biblical verses, which specifically delineate the divine intentional unity[17] that obtains between the Father and the Son. Conversely, Tertullian formulates the divine unity primarily in terms of intentionality and functionality: "By means of the works [performed by the Son], then, the Father will be in the Son and the Son in the Father, and thus by means of the works we understand that the Father and the Son are one" (*Adv Prax* 22.26–8). Utterly disregarding the intentional and functional unity (i.e. concord vis-à-vis purpose and work) of the Father and the Son, Satan attempts to overthrow God's truth by utilizing unsuspecting pawns like Praxeas to accomplish his ignoble ends.[18] For this reason, Tertullian is determined to expose the invidious demonic machinations actualized in the person of the Adversary's human agent, Praxeas.

Continuing with his vigorous polemic, Tertullian informs his readers that Praxeas relies on illegitimate appeals to scriptural references in the Fourth Gospel concerning the Father and Son's oneness so that he may establish his own peculiar form of Modalistic Monarchianism. Praxeas evidently conscripts Jn 10:30, *inter alia*, to buttress the notion that Jesus is hypostatically identical to the Father and as a result the Omnipotent Father incarnate. Yet, the implications of this daring theologumenon are quite stark since Praxeas' teaching implies that the Father "Himself came down into the virgin [Mary], Himself was born of her, Himself suffered, in short Himself is Jesus Christ" (*ipsum dicit patrem descendisse in virginem, ipsum ex ea natum, ipsum passum, denique ipsum esse Iesum Christum*).[19]

In contrast, Tertullian thinks the concept essayed by Praxeas is both logically absurd and scripturally untenable. The Praxean notion of deity also militates against the antiquitous "rule of faith" (*regula fidei*)[20] that the apostles supposedly handed down (*tradere*) to the ancient congregation of God.[21] The majority of post-Nicenes concur with Tertullian's theological assessment. These theologians later employed elements of the apologist's pistic defense in order that they might further refine orthodox Christology and Trinitarianism in the face of similar heresiarchal challenges to the church.[22] But Tertullian's theological rejoinder contra Praxeas has only just begun. Maurice Wiles aptly recapitulates the powerful effect that section (*caput*) one of *Adversus Praxean* commonly has on its readers when he writes: "The heart of his attack upon Praxeas is summed up in the jibe that his theology involved the blasphemous concept that the Father was crucified. This was the shaft that went home more surely than any other."[23] Indeed the charge of Patripassianism was enough to render the heresy of Praxeas essentially inoperative in the eyes of most readers, no doubt. Nonetheless, Tertullian does not desist with the forceful contention that Praxean Christology implies finite and lowly mortals put the transcendent and unapproachable God and Father of Jesus Christ to death.[24] To the contrary, in the following manner, Tertullian continues to build his case against the one whom he believes is the Devil's pliable minion.

C. TERTULLIAN'S EXTENDED CASE AGAINST PRAXEAS

Tertullian, still focusing on the tested wiles of the Devil as well as his propensity to subvert Christian truth by dissimulating a defense in its behalf, insists that if the Adversary really thinks the Father is also the Son, he possesses a faulty memory in light of the extant narratives of Christ's earthly life. The two Synoptic Gospels of Matthew and Luke[25] both record the Devil openly acknowledging the filial status of the Lord Jesus Christ[26] during the time that He temporarily dwelled among humanity:

> The serpent has forgotten himself: for when he tempted Jesus Christ after the baptism of John it was as Son of God that he attacked him, being assured that God has a Son at least from those very scriptures out of which he was then constructing the temptation.[27]

Tertullian then proceeds to quote Ps 91:11–12 (the verse that Satan utilized when attempting to deceive Jesus of Nazareth). He consequently reasons that the Devil either misspoke when he called Jesus God's Son or else the Synoptic Gospels Matthew and Luke composed wrongfully misrepresent the Devil—a thought that Tertullian is utterly unwilling to countenance for even one moment. The apologist accuses both the Devil and Praxeas of blatant disingenuousness. Moreover, he unambiguously maintains that both deceptive and spiritually malignant entities are exceedingly culpable before God since the Adversary has evidently inspired Praxeas to drive out prophecy and simultaneously crucify the Father (*ita duo negotia diaboli Praxeas Romae procuravit, prophetiam expulit et haeresim intulit, paracletum fugavit et patrem crucifixit*).[28] Therefore, while *Adversus Praxean* seems primarily concerned with the Praxean teaching of Patripassianism (the doctrine that God the Father became His own Son and subsequently suffered and died at Calvary in the first century of our common era), we need to say a brief word here about the purported heresiarch's efforts to expel prophecy from Rome.

It may be significant that Tertullian mentions the expulsion of prophecy before the crucifixion of the Father. Maybe this dubious act of Praxeas loomed larger in his mind than the threat of Patripassianism did. Tertullian relates that

Praxeas "drove out prophecy" in that he "put to flight the Paraclete" *(prophetiam expulit et haeresim intulit, paracletum fugavit)*.[29] In what sense did he drive out prophecy and chase away the Paraclete?

D. THE PRAXEAN ATTEMPT TO EXPEL PROPHECY FROM ROME

Earlier in *Adv Prax* 1, Tertullian chronicled how Rome's bishop was on the verge of acknowledging the charismatic prophecies that Montanus (fl. 170 CE), Prisca and Maximilla articulated until Praxeas began to promulgate fabricated reports concerning the Montanist spokespersons and their respective churches.[30] Montanus[31] appears to have believed that the Johannine promises concerning the Paraclete sent from the Father through the Son were uniquely fulfilled in him (Jn 14:16; 15:26; 16:7-13). Nevertheless, Montanus did not think that he was hypostatically or ontologically identical with the Holy Spirit or God.[32] All the same, the influential charismatic was eschatologically oriented, being ostensibly "gifted with visions and special revelations" that shaped his doctrine of the last things.[33] Tertullian testifies to the prophetic tendencies of the Cataphrygians, as opponents also called the Montanists, writing:

> Likewise the holy prophetess Prisca preaches that the holy minister should know how to administer purity of life. "For purification produces harmony," she says, "and they see visions, and when they turn their faces downward they also hear salutary voices, as clear as they are secret."[34]

The divine spirit manifested in visions, oracles and Scripture evidently inspired the Montanists to believe that the New Jerusalem foretold in John's Apocalypse (Apoc 21:1-2) would descend from heaven to Pepuza in their lifetime: "In view of this,

Christians should dissolve the bonds of wedlock, fast strictly and assemble in Pepuza to await the descent of the New Jerusalem."[35] The Montanists were ecstatic, hearing "salutary voices" (*etiam voces audiunt salutatares*) obscure in content but pellucid in tone. In view of the group's stress on holiness and divine inspiration, we are justified in asking what Praxean accusations irreparably tarnished the movement's image in the eyes of Rome's bishop.

As indicated above, the most intimate disciples of Montanus were women, and these feminine adherents filled rather prominent prophetic roles in the Montanist camp.[36] Montanus' willingness to use females in his eschatological group, however, undoubtedly contributed to complaints that suggested the prominent leader ruined marriages or wrongly appointed women to high-ranking ecclesiastical offices. H. O. J. Brown reports that Montanus thought marriages already consummated should be dissolved and marriages that were about to take place postponed since the end of the age was imminent. When the New Jerusalem did not descend as expected, Montanus and his disciples "broadened" the notion of the Last Day into "a concept of Last Days, during which Montanus called upon his followers to live a life of strict discipline and self-denial."[37] Of course, orthodoxy also had to adjust its eschatological outlook in view of the seeming delay of the Messiah's parousia. Individual eschatology thus gained greater prominence in orthodox circles.

Enemies of the eschatological movement further accused Montanus of "handling large sums of money" and paying his fellow visionaries hefty stipends.[38] While certain accusations directed at the Montanus probably had merit, "Some of the orthodox smears on him are manifest inventions."[39] Paul Johnson fittingly concludes that individuals such as Prisca and Maximilla were likely genuine, holy, meek and self-restrained believers that certain members of orthodoxy simply misunderstood.[40] Such "manifest inventions," however, appear to have been employed with some frequency against alleged heretical groups in the early church period.[41] The fact is that the Montanists unfortunately belonged to a group of persons that moderns collectively classify as the other,[42] a detail that Tertullian outlines in the opening *caput* of *Adversus Praxean*. The Praxean reports conveyed to the then ruling bishop of Rome were unmistakably scurrilous and probably lacking in probative truth-value. They too were undoubtedly "manifest inventions" that exposed the Cataphrygians to undeserved ill treatment and marginalization, *inter alia*.[43]

The Roman bishop, having heard such scandalous rumors about Montanus and his followers, promptly recalled the pacific missives that he had earlier dispatched and immediately expressed his manifest disapprobation of the Montanists. Consequently, injurious "false assertions" (*falsa de ipsis prophetis et ecclesiis eorumadseverando et praecessorum eius auctoritates defendendo coegit*)[44] concerning the New Prophecy (*nova prophetia*) earned Praxeas what seems to have been merited condemnation from the person of Tertullian. Moreover, Tertullian argued that the Praxean willingness to malign sincere, abstemious, and disciplined visionaries served as further evidence that he inadvertently accomplished "two pieces of the devil's business" in Rome (*ita duo negotia diaboli Praxeas Romae procuravit*).[45] Thence while the crucifixion of the Father may function as the focal point of Tertullian's assault on Praxeas, his concern over the coerced flight of the Paraclete is also evident in subsequent sections of

Adversus Praxean. Indeed, it may be a prominent concern in this work. With an overview of *caput* 1, however, we will now summarize Tertullian's argument contra Praxeas before examining the content of his particular brand of Christology.

FINDINGS

(1) Tertullian takes issue with Praxean theology for the following three reasons. First, Praxeas' doctrine of Christ unintentionally results in the crucifixion of the Father (Patripassianism).[46] Bart Ehrman highlights what Tertullian found objectionable about Praxean Christology as follows:

> Christ was divine, and as such his activities could be attributed to God; but he was not himself God the Father. The fine line [between Patripassianism and Adoptionism] can be detected in a careful thinker like Tertullian, who in one context refers to God as crucified (*De Carne* 5) but in another ridicules Praxeas for crucifying the Father (*Adv. Prax.* 1).[47]

Tertullian maintained that the impassible God and Judge of all could not suffer or undergo death on a humanly created *crux*. He carefully distinguished between the transcendent God and Christ, whom he associated with God since He emanated from God's *substantia*. Praxeas, however, failed to make the crucial hypostatic distinction between Christ and God the Father. For this reason, Tertullian felt compelled to write an entire treatise disposing of his propagated teaching that seemed to go well beyond the bounds of orthodoxy.

(2) Tertullian believes that orthodox Christianity's account of God and His Son accords with the long established rule of faith handed down to the nascent Christian congregation.[48] The ardent African's formulation of the *regula fidei* may differ from other versions of the so-called rule of faith, but Morgan points out that the *prima facie* disparateness of Tertullian's articulation of the *regula fidei* is a result of the pre-Nicene lack of emphasis on memorizing symbolic or creedal phrases *ad verbum*. Rather, the pre-Nicenes saw fit to stress concepts that early *symbola* communicated.[49] Even the famed Symbol of Nicea was "loosely quoted in later years."[50] Basing his pronouncements on the antiquity of apostolic belief, Tertullian consequently reasons that "whatever is earliest is true and whatever is later is counterfeit."[51] He indefatigably exalts what he thinks is the primordial apostolic Christological proclamation (κερυγμα) in his polemic against Praxeas.[52]

(3) Finally, Tertullian argues that Praxeas erroneously rejects the divine economy (*oikonomia*). Offering a riposte to his opponent, Tertullian retorts that although God is one vis-à-vis His substance or divine being, He "disposes the unity into Trinity" in order to redeem humankind.[53] But the plurality manifested in salvation history (*Heilsgeschichte*) does not admit division with respect to God's unitive substance since family connections (*pignora*) do not necessarily dissolve God's solitary rule (*monarchia*) anymore than a king's regal and filial officials undermine his sovereign sphere of influence, Tertullian concludes.

Tertullian's opening argument contra his formidable adversary seems to drive a lethal shaft into the Monarchian Christology of Praxeas. Even so, the apologist deems it necessary to marshal further evidence against his influential adversary. We will witness his potent rational demonstrations as we now progress to a discussion of sections (*capita*) 5–7 of *Adversus Praxean*. The primary reason for examining these particular *capita* will be to elucidate the *differentiae* between the eternal Logos-Sofia and the temporal Son *qua* Son. Making this epistemological distinction will prove to be vital when we review Tertullian's exegesis of Ps 8:5. Additionally, understanding the ontic disparity[54] between the Son *qua* Son and the expressed Logos will elucidate Tertullian's motivation for believing that the pre-existent and pre-angelophanic Son is lower than the angels.

NOTES

1. *Adversus Omnes Haereses* 8.4 by Pseudo-Tertullian reads: "Sed post hos omnes etiam Praxeas quidam haeresim introduxit, quam Victorinus corroborare curavit. Hic deum patrem omnipotentem Iesum Christum esse dicit, hunc crucifixum passumque contendit et mortuum, praeterea se ipsum sibi sedere ad dexteram suam, cum prophana et sacrilega temeritate proponit."

2. Evans, *Adversus Praxean*, 184.

3. Ibid. 185.

4. *Adv Prax* 1.

5. Ibid. 1.21–22" Nam iste primus ex Asia hoc genus perversitatis intulit Romam. Daniélou suggests that the type of Monarchianism espoused by Tertullian's antagonist, Praxeas, evidently originated in "Judaeo-Christian circles" moving about in the proximity of Asia Minor (*History of Early Church Doctrine*, 3:157).

6. Barnes recounts that though one can detect a number of theological similarities between Callistus and Tertullian's Praxeas, when it comes to the exact identity of Tertullian's adversary, "Certainty is unattainable" (*Tertullian*, 279). Barnes considers the moniker "Praxeas" a Greek *nom de plume* meaning "busybody." Conversely, Hall suggests that the name Praxeas means "fixer" or "fraud" in *Doctrine and Practice*, 70. He also submits that Praxeas may have been a subtle reference to Irenaeus since the bishop of Lyons was a noted opponent of Montanism and possibly an advocate of modalism (ibid).

7. Kelly, *Early Christian Doctrine*, 121.

8. Ibid. Cf. *Adv Prax* 21.

9. The first writer to state this belief in formal terms was Noetus of Smyrna (J. Kelly, *Early Christian Doctrine*, 120).

10. Frend, *The Rise of Christianity*, 344.

11. Ibid.

12. Edmund Fortman. *The Triune God: A Historical Study of the Doctrine of the Trinity* (Eugene: Wipf and Stock, 1999) 117.

13. Chadwick, *The Early Church*, 88.
14. Ibid.
15. *Adv Prax* 1.1.
16. Ibid.
17. Early church fathers such as Tertullian, Novatian and Hippolytus explained Jn 10:30 in terms of intentional or functional concord (i.e. unity as to purpose or intent): "We become one virtually, by our disposition towards singlemindedness. Well, in the same way the Son, sent and not recognized by those who are in the world, maintained that He is in the Father—virtually, as a disposition. For the Son is in the Father's 'single Mind,'" (*Contra Noet* 7.3).
18. Brown reports that Praxeas was evidently a *confessor*, that is, one who openly and resolutely confessed faith in Christ when summoned before prominent officials (i.e. judges). See *Heresies*, 100.
19. *Adv Prax* 1.7–8. Hippolytus (*Contra Noet* 3.2) relates that Theodotus the shoemaker (σκευτευς) "quite shamelessly" (αναιχυντος) stated: "The Father Himself is Christ; He is Himself the Son; He Himself was born, He Himself suffered, He Himself raised Himself up" (αυτος εστι χριστος ὁ πατηρ αυτος υιος αυτος εγεννθη αυτος επαθεν αυτος ἑαυτον γειρεν).
20. Appealing to the primary sources, Bray demonstrates that Tertullian uses the Latin *regula* to signify a summarization that Christ's followers can avail themselves of in order to understand and interpret Scripture (*Holiness and the Will of God*, 102–104).
21. See Rebecca Lyman's compact but insightful comments on the role of tradition and traditions in Christianity in *Early Christian Traditions* (Cambridge: Cowley, 1999), 3–8.
22. Pelikan develops this theme in *The Christian Tradition*, 1:172–277.
23. Maurice Wiles, *The Making of Chrstian Doctrine: A Study in the Principles of Early Doctrinal Development* (London: Cambridge University Press, 1967), 215.
24. Bethune-Baker deems Tertullian's inference from the Praxean self-identical divine modes of Being "unfair" and he points out that the so-called Patripassians themselves manifestly did not accept Tertullian's assumption, even if they did think Jesus Christ was identical with God (*Early History*, 103–104). There are, however, legitimate logical conundrums that attend Modalism. Bethune-Baker himself relates how difficult it is to account for the Modalistic thesis that says the Son as God suffers, although God is impassible.
25. Mt 4 and Lk 4.
26. Matthew's Synoptic account (4:5–6), according to the Vg reads: "Tunc assumit eum Diabolus in sanctam civitatem et statuit eum supra pinnaculum templi et dicit ei: 'Si Filius Dei es, mitte te deorsum. Scriptum est enim: Angelis suis mandabit de te, et in manibus tollent te, ne forte offendas ad lapidem pedem tuum.'"
27. *Adv Prax* 1.9–11: "Excidit sibi coluber, quia Iesum Christum post baptisma Ioannis temptans ut filium dei adgressus est, certus filium deum habere vel ex ipsis scripturis de quibus tunc temptationem struebat."
28. Ibid., 1.31–33.

29. Ibid.

30. Felicity and Perpetua were no doubt Montanists. See E. Evans, *Adversus Praxean*, 188. The Roman church has never discredited these matyrs. In this connection, Barnes also observes that Montanus embarked upon his prophetic career in 170 CE. Subsequent to this period, the New Prophecy spread rapidly and almost gained favorable recognition from the church. Barnes concludes: "There is no reason entirely to disbelieve the explicit statement of Tertullian that the bishop of Rome recognized the prophecies of Montanus, Prisca and Maximilla as genuine utterances of the Holy Spirit, and was on the point of communicating his acceptance to the churches of Asia and Phrygia" (*Tertullian*, 82). Barnes additionally confirms that the rumors purportedly propagated by Praxeas concerning the Montanists were indeed fictitious. Nevertheless, the New Prophecy actually remained "acceptable" even after the year 203 CE. Yet, evidently because of the Roman bishop's disapprobation toward Montanism, believers in Carthage began to defect from the ecstatic movement (*Tertullian*, 83).

31. Olson reports that Montanus was a "pagan priest" in Asia Minor (Phrygia) before he became a Christian in the middle part of the second-century. See *Story of Christian Theology*, 31. Montanus' turning point vis-à-vis his relationship with the church seems to have been his insistence that the bishops do not have divinely ordained "special authority" (ibid).

32. Pelikan thinks that the concept of the Johannine Paraclete actually played an insignificant role in early Montanism. He also notes that Montanus did not believe that he himself was the Paraclete per se, but that God's Παρακλητος worked through him in the sense that it divinely influenced Montanus. However, Pelikan's position is clearly at odds with Epiphanius' statements in *Panarion* 48.11.

In any event, it is difficult to determine when Tertullian uses the word Paraclete to reference Montanus and when he is using it to signify the Holy Spirit. See Pelikan, *The Christian Tradition*, 1:102–104. Cf. Eusebius' H.E. 5.16.17.

On the other hand, Tabbernee relates that the term Paraclete used with reference to the Holy Spirit, was not exclusively confined to the Montanists. An inscription that is supposed to be Montanist in nature which employs the term Paraclete may well be Donatist in origin according to *Montanist Inscriptions*, 543–544. For more evidence suggesting Montanus did not think he was a human manifestation of the Paraclete, see ibid. 32–33. Cf. Aune, *Prophecy*, 314–315.

33. Pelikan, *The Christian Tradition*, 1:102–104.

34. *De exhortatione* 10.5. Cited in Heine, *Montanist Oracles*, 4–5: "Item per sanctam prophetidem Priscam ita evangelizatur, quod sanctus minister sanctimoniam noverit ministrare. Purificantia enim concordat, ait, et visiones vident, et ponentes faciem deorsum etiam voces audiunt salutares, tam manifestas quam et occultas."

35. Reinhold Seeberg, *Textbook of the History of Doctrines,* trans. Charles E. Hay (Grand Rapids: Baker Book House, 1966), 105; Aune, *Prophecy*, 313. Pepuza, a town located in Phrygia, was the place where Montanus and the two principal female spokespersons of the New Prophecy constructed their "commune." See Olson, *Story of Theology*, 31. Therefore, it was only fitting that the New Jerusalem would descend there.

36. Pagels, *Gnostic Gospels*, 60. Tertullian also provides evidence of Montanus' willingness to use women ecclesiastically in *De Anima* 9. There, he speaks about the charismatic experiences of one female Cataphrygian.

37. Brown, *Heresies*, 67.

38. Paul Johnson, *A History of Christianity* (New York and London: Simon Schuster, 1976), 49.

39. Ibid.

40. Ibid. 50.

41. For similar cases, consult Pagels' *Gnostic Gospels*.

42. Insightfully, Terry Eagleton describes the other as not just a "theoretical concept" but an actual category delineating movements or peoples "written out of history, subjected to slavery, insult, mystification, genocide" in his work *Literary Theory: An Introduction* (Minneapolis: University of Minnesota Press, 1998), 205.

43. Olson's account of the Montanists is not quite as sympathetic as Johnson's. He locates the root of the Montanists' troubles in their open defiance of bishops ruling throughout the Roman Empire. Furthermore, Montanus claimed to be the especial instrument through which God's Holy Spirit spoke, an assertion that placed Catholic claims in serious jeopardy. This is the proposal of Olson, *Story of Theology*, 32. See Hall, *Doctrine and Practice*, 46–47. Nonetheless, there appears to be little substance to the "inventions" that Johnson and Olson discuss.

44. *Adv Prax* 1.28–30.

45. Ibid. 1.32.

46. Apology 1.127.

47. Ehrman, *Orthodox Corruption*, 87.

48. Metzger explains that the *regula fidei* signifies that which has been orally transmitted by the apostles and received or handed down by the church. The rule of faith is: "the immemorial belief of Christians, derived from the Scriptures" and that content set forth in the Apostles' Creed (Metzger, *Canon*, 158).

49. Kelly also observes that the "rule of faith" (*regula fidei*) is "the intrinsic shape and pattern" of God's revelation to the apostles. The *regula* is supposed to function as the basis for an accurate interpretation of the holy writings (Kelly, *Early Christian Doctrines*, 40). Macquarries writes that Scripture "comes alive only in the ongoing life of the community, which first gave birth to scripture [sic] and has since proclaimed and interpreted the teaching of scripture." See *Principles of Christian Theology* (New York: Charles Scribner's Sons, 1977). 11.

50. Morgan, *The Importance of Tertullian*, 49. Cf. appendix I.

51. *Adv Prax* 2. Robert Wilken, *The Myth of Christian Beginnings* (London: SCM Press, 1979) 47–51 illustrates how the claim "truth is older than error" was not restricted to Christianity since the entire Greco-Roman world stressed the importance of tradition and antiquity. The Romans even emphasized the importance of ancestral custom *(mos maiorum)* as part of a proper formal education. At any rate, "Tradition," writes Wilken, "needed no justification; it authenticated itself simply by being old. Antiquity itself was a sign of truth, for what is older is better." Obviously, such a view

was not meant to serve as a strict logical form of argumentation. Tertullian was simply appealing to a notion that permeated the spirit of the times (*Zeitgeist*).

52. Grillmeier, *Christ in Christian Tradition*, 140.

53. *Adv Prax* 2.

54. We are using the term "ontic" here to signify particular beings over against ontological universals.

Chapter Four

The Distinction between the Sermo Dei and Son qua Son

In order to understand the basis for Tertullian's belief that the pre-existent Son *qua* Son was lower than the angels in station and possibly being, it is necessary to make certain vital distinctions between the *ratio* and *filius dei*. A failure to discern such ontic differentiations may explain why some commentators insist that Tertullian posits an eternal *generatio* for the pre-eminent Son of God.[1] However, the evidence from *Adversus Praxean* appears to suggest otherwise: Tertullian believes that God generated the Son *in tempo*.

The author of the treatise against Praxeas presents an extended description of the *ratio, sermo et filius dei* in *capita* 5–8 of *Adversus Praxean*. We will first identify how he makes use of these terms vis-à-vis Christ before we proceed with a discussion of the biblical exegesis set forth in Tertullian's work opposing Praxean Christology.

A. RATIO

Lewis and Short provide a useful definition for *ratio* that helps us to discern how Tertullian employs the term in his polemic contra Praxeas. Acording to this classical source, *ratio* can refer to "that faculty of the mind which forms the basis of computation and calculation, and hence of mental action in general, i. e. judgment, understanding, reason." This lexical delineation[2] of the Latin signifier appropriately describes how Tertullian utilizes the word *ratio* with reference to God. He essentially conceives of the *ratio dei* as the immanent thought or impersonal reason of God. This impersonal divine ratiocinating faculty ultimately becomes a relational or personal agent in the form of God's Son.

The Greek equivalent of *ratio* is Λογος. Greek philosophers sometimes employ this signifier to describe an "aspect" of God, namely, a divine emanation or effluence that is simultaneously an individuated deific hypostasis.[3] In the Stoicism of Zeno, for example, Λογος is the "divine word."[4] One difficulty, however, is that, "The Romans were unable to translate *logos* with one term."[5] Therefore, Latins embraced the phrase *ratio et ratio* (reason and speech) to make the signification of Logos clear to non-Greek speakers. Latin speakers thus associated thought and speech with the concept of *ratio*.[6] Nevertheless, Tertullian (who spoke Latin and also possessed a working knowledge of Greek) believed that humans are not the only beings, who possess the faculty of reason since God is the supreme locus of rationality: "The God of biblical revelation is the God of reason, not Ultimate Irrationality; all he does is rational."[7]

Tertullian indicates that God is not "Ultimate Irrationality." Reason is one of His objective and eternal or everlasting properties. Nevertheless, if reason is a divine property, it seems one can justly infer that the Most High determined and created everything by means of His own expressed *ratio* (Λογος προφορικος). Tertullian possesses just such a view of the created cosmos as evidenced below:

> Reason, in fact, is a thing [property] of God, inasmuch as there is nothing which God the Maker of all has not provided, disposed, ordained by reason-nothing which He has not willed should be handled and understood by reason.[8]

Furthermore, Tertullian refers to the *ratio dei* as a divine attribute or property in *Adversus Praxean*. There was a time, however, when the Son of God as Son did not exist; nor was God always a Father (*Adv Herm* 3.18). Conversely, *ratio* is an eternal quality of deity. Through His own reason (*ratio*), the Most High produced the cosmos and all that is therein. Hence, based on Tertullian's account, we must make an ontic distinction between the *ratio dei* that did not come into existence but eternally subsisted in God and the *filius dei* that came into being to mediate the divine *creatio ex nihilo*.

B. SERMO

Tertullian also uses *sermo* to translate the Greek Λογος. Evans usually renders *sermo* as "Discourse." It is indeed significant that the noted church apologist opts for the Latin *sermo* (Discourse) instead of *verbum* (word), implying that God mentally discourses with Himself in eternity and does not simply articulate a mere word while subsisting as the sole personal agent in existence. Tertullian in this way emphasizes divine cognition *qua* interior discourse when he employs *sermo* throughout his writings. Ergo, we should not strictly correlate *sermo* with *filius* (referentially) when the subject of the former term is Jesus Christ. The importance of observing this distinction (between *sermo* and *filius*) will emerge later in this study.

C. SOPHIA

In *Adv Prax* 6 Tertullian reminds his opponent that God's consciousness is "in the Scriptures also displayed under the name of Wisdom" (*Haec vis et haec divini sensus dispositio apud scripturas etaim in sophiae nomine ostenditur*). As the Latin portion of this citation makes clear, Tertullian uses the Greek equivalent *Sophia* to represent Wisdom personified. The ancient writings of Judaism undoubtedly influence Tertullian's view of divine Wisdom. He appears to cull verses concerning this sapiential figure from canonical, deuterocanonical, and pseudepigraphical sources.[9]

Regardless of the *locus classicus* for his doctrine of the *Sophia* figure familiar to both Judaism and Gnosticism, *Adv Prax* 6 reveals that Tertullian is primarily interested in harmonizing Christian teachings with the canonical writings of Judaism and Christianity. He clearly desires to meet his antagonist on the common ground of Holy Writ. Moreover, Tertullian employs texts such as Prov 8:22–31 to prove that the Logos became a Son to God *in tempo*: "Discourse, who became Son of God when by proceeding from Him He was begotten" (*qui filius factus est dei, de quo prodeundo generatus est*).[10] This "perfect nativity of Discourse" (*nativitas perfecta sermonis*) was in fact the beginning of the Son's minoration. The Father then temporally brought forth the pre-incarnate Son.

The previously mentioned passage found in Tertullian (*Adv Prax* 7.1) highlights both the differentiation and minoration of the Son in relation to the Father. As we will learn below, the Son's generation also makes it possible for Christ to be functionally minor with respect to the angels. However, for now, it is sufficient to note that Tertullian avails himself of the term *Sophia* to delineate the immanent divine reason, which God begets for the sake of creation, in order that it may become His expressed Word (Λογος προφορικος).[11]

D. DISTINGUISHING THE ETERNAL RATIO FROM THE TEMPORAL FILIUS

Tertullian seeks to establish that the Son and Father are not hypostatically identical by directing attention to the holy scriptures of Judaism and Christianity.

He is eager to establish his case forensically: "by the advocacy of the scriptures and the interpretations of them" (*et ita res ipsa formam suam scripturis et interpretationibus earum patrocinantibus vindicabit*).[12] He therefore places a similar challenge before his formidable opponent, declaring: "But it will be your duty to prove it [Monarchianism] as openly from the scriptures as we prove that He made His own Word His Son" (*Probare autem tam aperte debebis ex scripturis quam nos probamus illum sibi filium fecisse sermonem suum*).[13] The apologist is accordingly intent on substantiating his belief from Scripture (both the OT and NT). He consequently turns the tables on his antagonist with polished and skilled shrewdness. While Praxeas supposedly employs Holy Writ to support his fabricated accusations against those, who adhere to the tenets of Montanism, the *vir ardens* from Carthage convincingly demonstrates that Praxeas neither rightly nor properly explicates God's Word of truth (2 Tim 2:15). Tertullian clearly and forcefully points out that Praxeas distorts the sacred writings of Christianity. The purported heresiarch is an unwitting satanic pawn trying to undermine Christian *veritas* by pretending to defend it. Conversely, Tertullian evidently substantiates his case by making a legitimate appeal to the Scriptures and invoking the *regula fidei*. We will now examine how he utilizes the holy writings of Judaism in his defense of Christian truth.

The first text that the skilled Christian rhetorician considers is Gen 1:1: "In the beginning, God created the heavens and the earth" (*In principio creavit Deus caelum et terram*). He then discloses that "certain people" think the primitive cosmic account contained in Moses' first pentateuchal book should actually read: "In the beginning God made for himself a Son" (*aiunt quidam et Genesim in Hebraico ita incipere in principio deus fecit sibi filium*).[14] However, Evans suggests that Tertullian has evidently "misunderstood his informant" since this imaginative reading does not seem to reoccur in other Patristic writings.[15] Bernard Lonergan, on the other hand, defends the reliability of Tertullian's report citing Clement of Alexandria (*Stromata* 6.7.58; 6.39.2), Jerome (*Quaest Hebr In Gen* 1:1),[16] and Irenaeus as sources that support Tertullian.[17]

In any event, Tertullian (for sound theological and textual reasons) appropriately rejects such a reading of Gen 1:1 and concludes that God subsisted in a solitary but self-sufficient or autarchic condition before the creation of the cosmos: "until the generation of the Son" (*fuit ante mundi constitutionem as usque filii generationem*).[18] This last sentence indicates that there was a time when God the Father was all alone, prior to the generation of the Son. Nevertheless, Evans thinks that this concept—God the Father subsisting without His Son (*filius*)—is utterly unthinkable. What does the evidence from *Adversus Praxean* suggests?

Evans states that Tertullian immediately corrects any possibility of misunderstanding what he writes concerning God's eternal pre-cosmic solitariness when he immediately qualifies his theological pronouncement by declaring: "Yet not even then was He alone" (*ceterum ne tunc quidem solus*).[19] Contra the eminent translator, however, we maintain that Tertullian believes the awe-inspiring God of Tertullian (who became the Father) was initially alone in a hypostatic sense, personally existing as a self-sufficient world to His own self, autarchically. Both Minucius Felix and Athenagoras of Antioch also seem to posit a solitary hypostatic deity who subsists alone before He generates the Logos as Son *qua* Son.[20] There thus appears to be ample historical evidence pointing to an early Christian belief that God was all alone (hypostatically) until He brought forth Discourse (*sermo*) to mediate creation.[21]

Granted, Tertullian explicitly states that God was alone since "there was nothing external beside him" (*solus autem quia nihil aliud extrinsecus praeter illum*), implying that there was possibly an entity internally adjacent to Him, namely, His own eternal reason (*ratio*).[22] Hence, one may be justified in concluding that Tertullian believed there was an eternal divine hypostasis existing internally next to God (the Father) before the creation of all things in the capacity of a relationally opposed subsistent. The context of *Adv Prax* 5, however, suggests a different understanding of matters.[23] We will now assess the evidence that indicates Tertullian does not think the *ratio dei* is an eternal *res et persona*.

Tertullian maintains that God (the Father) was (technically) not alone before He created the world since His own reason (*ratio*) eternally resided within Him. However, the ancient Carthaginian's main point here seems to be that in a manner analogous to humans participating in the act of inward discourse (i.e. reasoning), making themselves objects of contemplation to and for themselves, God from all eternity past, deliberated or ratiocinated interiorly. In this manner, the Christian deity made Himself the supreme object of contemplation for Himself.[24] Tertullian insists that such inward, rational discourse is apropos for the Most High God (*Summus Deus*): "For God is rational, and reason is primarily in Him, and thus from Him are all things: and that Reason is His consciousness" (*rationalis enim deus, et ratio in ipso prius, et ita ab ipso omnia: quae ratio sensus ipsius est*).[25] Yet the *ratio* internal beside God ante creation was not yet a *res et persona* (a particular object or objective personal presentation)[26] as Tertullian explains.[27]

Tertullian reasons that since humans are made in God's image (*imago dei*) and are rational beings[28] fashioned out of God's own substance[29] into living souls,[30] the activity that occurs when human cognizers through the act of contemplation "by reason argue silently"[31] resembles the pre-generational act of God whereby He "made another beside himself by activity within himself."

58   Chapter Four

That is, God made Reason (*ratio*) Discourse (*sermo*) and subsequently it became His own Son.³² The partner that one encounters in mental discourse, however, is neither an extra-mental (*extra mente*) reality nor an authentic person. One's inward discourse partner is only a *quasi persona*, not being a genuine hypostatic entity in relation. When one reflects *ad intra*, there is not another distinct *persona* within him or her. He or she only possesses a figurative interlocutor at such contemplative periods. Tertullian reinforces this point by penning the following words: "So in a sort of a way you have in you as a second <person> discourse by means of which you speak by thinking and by means of which you think by speaking: discourse itself is another <than you>."³³

Based on the foregoing data, we seem warranted in concluding that Tertullian believed that God the Father subsisted alone previous to the founding of the cosmos, with no other distinct *personae* internal or external beside Him. He simply possessed *ratio* (i.e. His own faculty of reason) or *sermo* (Discourse). Hence, the Latin apologist from North Africa notes that while God always had the potential for plurality or differentiation *in se*, He did not fully actualize this potential (*potentia*) until the complete nativity of the Word (*nativitas perfecta sermonis*).³⁴ That is why Tertullian could proclaim in yet another document: "There was, however, a time when neither sin existed with him, nor the Son" (*fuit autem tempus, cum et delictum et filius non fuit*)³⁵. Harnack expresses matters thus: "The *Logos* [according to Tertullian] came into existence as a real being, before the world and for the sake of the world."³⁶ The Latin apologist reasons that God became a Father to the Logos when He outwardly expressed Discourse qua Λογος προφορικος.

Concerning Tertullian's fuller statement of God's existence antecedent to the generation of His Son, Harnack perspicuously observes that although the *ratio et sermo dei* eternally resided within God since "he [God] thought and spoke inwardly," God (the Father) was still "the only person" in existence before the Son's begettal.³⁷ Edmund Fortman also reasons that the Son of God (according to Tertullian) "was generated, not from eternity but before and for creation, and then became a second person."³⁸ Preceding His *generatio*, however, Tertullian argues that Discourse was not "clearly and fully personalized."³⁹

Stead further discerns that Tertullian depicts God as an infinite mind (νουν) containing Word in the sense of "plan" or "thought" within it.⁴⁰ Moreover, he further states: "This latter is sufficiently distinct to be addressed as a 'partner in dialogue.'"⁴¹ Yet this *sermo* does not become Son until God utters the words, "Let there be light" (*fiat lux*) as recorded in Gen 1:3. Stead writes that Tertullian speaks of Discourse (*sermo*) as God's Son in the fullest sense when relating what God accomplished on the first creative day.⁴² It might, therefore, be inaccurate to argue that Tertullian thinks the Son is a timeless *res et persona* internal beside the supreme Monarch. This ancient writer inextricably associates the Son's hypostaticity with the *constitutionem mundi*.

FINDINGS

Earlier, in *Adv Prax* 11, we read that God made *sermo* His Son. The famous passage in *Adv Herm* 3.18 also affirms: "there was, however, a time when neither sin existed with him, nor the Son" (*fuit autem tempus, cum et delictum et filius non fuit*). These texts illustrate that there is a marked distinction between the Reason or Word of God (*ratio sive sermo dei*) and the Son *qua* Son. Whereas *ratio et sermo* are applied to the everlasting divine ratiocinating activity as immanent or expressed, Tertullian unequivocally reveals that there was not an eternal or timeless *res et persona* internally or externally next to God before the Most High made His own Word a Son to Him (*sibi filium fecisse sermonem suum*).[43] Ergo, Tertullian uses the word "Son" (*filius*) to describe the *ratio sive sermo dei* expressed as personalized and temporal *res*. Nevertheless, before the *nativitas perfecta sermonis*, the Logos, in the manner of ancient Judaism's *hokhmah* was simply the personification of a divine attribute or faculty.[44] Worded another way, the *Sermo dei* is not an eternal hypostasis or an eternal *res et persona*.

NOTES

1. Evans, *Adversus Praxean*, 224–225.
2. By ' lexical delineation," I simply have in mind, "the conventional meaning conveyed by the use of words and sentences in a language" See George Yule. *The Study of Language* (Cambridge: Cambridge University Press, 1996), 114. That is, according to the model being used in this study, meaning is largely a matter of convention. We say "largely" since the mental lexicon posited by psycholinguists also seems to play a part in determining the meaning of linguistic symbols. The present writer is also not averse to the thought of disembodied signfication that is *extra mente naturaliter*.
3. Edward V. Arnold, *Roman Stoicism: Being Lectures on the History of the Stoic Philosophy with Special Reference to Its Development within the Roman Empire* (Cambridge University Press, Cambridge, 1911), 12.
4. Ibid. 17.
5. Ibid. 37.
6. See Philo, *Vit Mos* 2.129.
7. Carl F. H. Henry, *God, Revelation*, and *Authority*, 4 vol. (Waco: Word, 1976), 1:232. See James E. White, *What is Truth?* (Nashville: Broadman and Holman, 1994), 103.

8. *De Paen* 1: "Ceterum a ratione eius tantum absunt quantum ab ipso rationis auctore. Quippe res dei ratio quia deus omnium conditor nihil non ratione providit disposuit ordinavit nihilque non ratione tractari intellegique voluit."

9. See Daniélou, *History of Early Church Doctrine*, 3:161–173.

10. *Adv Prax* 7.1.

11. O'Collins, *The Tripersonal God*, 108.

12. *Adv Prax* 5.

13. *Adv Prax* 11.1.

14. *Ibid.* 5.9–11.

15. Evans, *Adversus Praxean*, 209.

16. Marcel Simon also supplies evidence for the reading cited by Tertullian in *The Bible in Greek Christian Antiquity*, trans. Paul M. Blowers (Notre Dame: University of Notre Dame Press, 1997), 62.

17. See Lonergan, *The Way to Nicea: The Dialectical Development of Trinitarian Theology*, trans. Conn O'Donovan (London: Dartman, Longman, and Todd, 1976), 23–4. *VL* reads: "In principio fecit deus caelum et terram. The Latin Vg says: In principio creavit Deus caelum et terram."

18. *Adv Prax* 5.12–13.

19. Ibid. 5.15.

20. In *Adv Prax* 5, Tertullian writes: For before all things God was alone, He was a world and place and all things" (ante omnia enim deus erat solus, ipse sibi et mundus et locus et omnia). In *Octavius* 18.7, Minucius expresses the following viewpoints: "Before the world, he was a world to himself" (ante mundum fuerit sibi ipse pro mundo) and "By his word he orders all things that exist, by means of his reason he arranges them and by his perfect goodness he perfects them" (Verbo iubet, ratione dispensat, virtute consummat). See Daniélou, *History of Early Church Doctrine*, 3:190. Similarly, Athenagoras writes: "You sovereigns, indeed, rear and adorn your palaces for yourselves; but the world was not created because God needed it; for God is Himself everything to Himself, light unapproachable, a perfect world, spirit, power, reason." (*Leg pro* 16). The context suggests that the God Athenagoras has in mind is the one who, according to Tertullian, becomes a Father to the Logos. Municius Felix seems to have the same referent in mind.

21. Cyril C. Richardson, *The Doctrine of the Trinity* (New York: Abingdon, 1958), 57.

22. *Adv Prax* 5.14–17.

23. Tatian provides a similar account of the pre-cosmic *Sitz-im-Leben* of the Father and Son: "The Lord of all things who was himself the foundation of the whole was alone in relation to the creation which had not yet come into being" ὁ γαρ δεσποτης των ὁλων αυτος 'υπαρχων του παντος ὑποστασις κατα μεν την μηδεπω γεγενημενην ποιησιν μονος ἠν. See *Oratio* 5.16–21. Nevertheless, Tatian makes it clear that the pre-generated Logov is not a divine *persona*. In both Tatian and Tertullian, the pre-generated Logos is God's rational power.

24. Adolf Harnack, *History of Dogma, trans. Neil Buchanan*, 7 vols. (New York: Dover, 1961), 2:259. In order to help us somewhat grasp the workings of the divine precosmic rationating activity, Tertullian, anticipating the later Augustine (*De Trin*

VIII–XV), asks us to reflect on the inner discourse (i.e. discursive activities) that take place in the human mind.

25. *Adv Prax* 5.17–18.

26. George L. Prestige, *God in Patristic Thought* (London: SPCK, 1969), 221.

27. We find a similar Logos theory posited in Hippolytus. According to the apologetic writer based in Rome, God once existed alone, having nothing contemporaneous with himself (*Contra Noet* 10.1–2). Hippolytus, however, declares that "alone though he was" God was "manifold" (αυτος δε μονος ων πολυς 'ῃ) in that "he was not Word-less (ουτε αλογος) nor Wisdom-less (ουτε ασοφος) nor Power-less (ουτε αδυνατος) nor Mind-less (ουτε αβουλευτος). But everything was in him, and he was himself the All." The previously mentioned delineation outlined by Hippolytus suggests that the Λογος residing in God from all eternity was not a *res* or distinct *persona*. Furthermore, God wills the Logos into existence (*Contra Noet* 10.3). This aspect of Hippolytus' theory is seemingly problematic for Trinitarians since it implies that the Son is not an essential divine hypostasis. See Fortman, *Triune God*, 118. If Hippolytus is correct, then the Logos become Son (even prior to His enfleshment) is a creature temporarily and arbitrarily deified for a short period of time. See Frend, *The Rise of Christianity*, 344–345. Fortman carefully delineates both the impersonal and subsequent personal stages of the Logos in *The Triune God*, 118.

28. The tradition of man subisting as a rational being can be found in the Stoic and Aristotelian traditions. Clement of Alexandria also thought that man is the image of God in that he is rational (λογικος): "Hence, man is God's image by virtue of his mind (nouv), his reasoning faculty, not because of any sensible, to say nothing of anatomical, resemblance," See William E. G. Floyd, *Clement of Alexandria's Treatment of the Problem of Evil* (London: Oxford University Press, 1971), 20.

29. Evans tries to downplay Tertullian's language here by noting that the apologist uses *ex* when referring to the Son's generation from God's substance and *de* when talking about humanity. However, we are not so sure that Tertullian has such prepositional distinctions in mind. For he employs *ex* and *de* interchangeably with reference to the Son's *derivatio* from the *substantia* of the Father.

30. *Adv Prax* 5.32–34: "Tu in timetipso rationem qui es animal rationale, a rationali scilicet artifice non tantum factus sed etiam ex substantia ipsius animatus."

31. Ibid. 5.34–35.

32. Ibid. 5.12–13.

33. "Ita secundus quoammodo in te est sermo per quem loqueris cogitando et per quem cogitas loquendo: ipse sermo alius est."

34. One can read about the perfect nativity of the Son in *Adv Prax* 7.34–35. Tertullian's God is not the deity of Thomas Aquinas. He is not strictly pure act (*actus purus*), since it is possible for Him to have unactualized potential so to speak. Nor is Tertullian's God fully impassible, since He is ontologically mutable. For instance, He becomes a Father and expresses emotions the Thomist deity seems incapable of showing. See John Sanders, *The God Who Risks: A Theology of Providence* (Downers Grove: InterVarsity Press, 1998), 143.

35. *Adv Herm* 3.18.

36. Harnack, *History of Dogma*, 2.259. Tatian's Logos theology is based on similar notions. Tatian's doctrine of the Λογος corresponds with Justin Martyr's, for the most part. He loves to speak of the Word in terms of "Logos-Potency" (λογου δυναμιν) or *potentia*. This Word of God is first immanent in the Omnipotent deity but in time becomes the agent of creation as well as God's personal agent of revelation. Logov is depicted in Tatian as ìthe Divine Reason considered as potentially capable of acting in conditions wherein the Transcendent Father does not move, viz: in the phenomenal world which the Logos originates as the Father's intermediary." See Spence Little, *The Christology of the Apologists*: (London: Duckworth, 1934), 181–182. The Logos, as the rational potentiality of the Father, contains creation within itself ideally. The Word springs forth in a manner analogous to reason emanating from the human mind (ibid. 183–184). Moreover, the Logos in Tatian is an abstract conception of divine rationality that assumes hypostaticity prior to and for the purpose of creation. The criticisms of Irenaeus and Hippolytus directed toward Tatian may therefore be justified. See *Adv Haer* I, 28 and *Philosophumena* 8.16.

37. Harnack, *History of Dogma*, 2:259.

38. *The Triune God*, 111.

39. Ibid.

40. *Divine Substance*, 228. Sydney Mellone writes: "Tertullian holds that the term *Logos* is a legitimate metaphor involving a vital truth, because the Greek term *Logos* and the Latin *Sermo* (used as its equivalent) imply both a necessary distinction and a necessary relation between the thought or reason and its expression" (*Leaders*, 122).

41. Stead, *Divine Substance*, 228.

42. Ibid.

43. *Adv Prax* 11.

44. Pagels, *Gnostic Gospels*, 53–54 discusses the Gnostic characterization of the divine mother in the πληρωμα as σοφια. Pagels then recounts how early Gnostic interpreters often wondered if scriptural texts that discuss God creating the world in wisdom (Prov 3 and 8) meant that God "conceived" creation using a feminine cosmic principle. Valentinus also employed the σοφια motif to explain the manner in which lady Wisdom became the "Mother of all living" sans a masculine cosmic principle.

Chapter Five

Tertullian's Exegesis of Ps 8:5 in Adversus Praxean

In a previous chapter, we evaluated every pre-Nicene occurrence of Ps 8:5. We then learned that Tertullian only applies the hymnodic song of praise found in the eighth psalm to the Messiah. However, he believes that there are three distinct ways in which the Son became lower than angels. *Sermo* became inferior to the angels when it developed into God's Son.[1] That is, when God spoke the words, "*fiat lux*," He made the impersonal *ratio dei* His own Son.[2] Furthermore, when the Son of God appeared in OT angelophanies, He condescended or humbled Himself, thereby making himself lower than the angels.[3] Lastly, the Father makes the Son lower than the angels when Christ assumes flesh. Now that we have evaluated the foregoing exegetical construals of Tertullian in a general manner, we will specifically consider how Tertullian explains the relevance of Ps 8:5 in his momentous theological treatise, *Adversus Praxean*.

A. THE PREEXISTENT SON AND ADVERSUS PRAXEAN 9

Praxeas maintains that the Father, Son, and Holy Spirit are hypostatically indistinguishable. In other words, the deific subsistencies (*subsistentiae*) of the Trinity are purportedly three successive modes of the same divine person. Theologians generally label this view, "Monarchianistic Modalism." Tertullian deems this theological notion heretical, and the church in due course agreed with him. To combat Praxeas' Modalistic Christology, Tertullian avers:

> For look now, I say that the Father is one, and the Son another, and the Spirit another (every unlearned or self-willed person takes this statement in bad part, as

though it proclaimed diversity and because of diversity threatened a separation of Father and Son and Spirit: but I am bound to make it, so long as they maintain that Father and Son and Spirit are identical, favouring the monarchy at the expense of the economy), not however that the Son is other than the Father by diversity, but by distribution, not by division but by distinction, because the Father is not identical with the Son, they even being numerically one and another.[4]

Kelly remarks that even in Justin's day, there were reports of certain Christians who objected to the teaching that the Logos is "something numerically other" (αριθμαί ἕτερον τί) than the Father (*Dial* 128.3).[5] Tertullian also states that the "simple people" (*simplices*) of his time, a term that could simply refer to catechumenates and not unlearned followers of Christ *per se*, whom he insists always constitute the majority of God's worshipers, did not grasp that they must believe God is both one and three according to the dispensation of the economy (*dispositio oikonomiae*).[6]

Tertullian argues that the Father, Son, and Holy Spirit are distinct, diverse, and differentiated Persons since they are putatively three opposed relations. Yet, the *tres personae* do not experience abscission in relation to the divine substance. Tertullian thereby tries to concurrently uphold the divine monarchy and economy. Conversely, he declares that the "unlearned" (*simplices*) believers of his time unwarrantedly reject God's economic threeness in favor of His immanent and eternal oneness. They do not comprehend, Tertullian asseverates, in what manner the Father is identical to the Son and differentiable from Him since they place too much emphasis on the Monarchy:

> For all the simple people, that I say not the thoughtless and ignorant (who are always the majority of the faithful), since the rule of the Faith itself brings <us> over from the many gods of the world to the one only true God, not understanding that while they must believe in one only <God> yet they must believe in him along with his economy, shy at the economy. They claim that the plurality and ordinance of trinity is a division of unity—although a unity which derives from itself a trinity is not destroyed but administered by it.[7]

The Son is other than the Father by "distribution" (*distributione*) and "distinction" (*distinctione*). *Distributio* "appears to mean an assignment, or allocation, of functions (and so forth) among persons fundamentally alike."[8] It is an overlapping relation (i.e. synonym) of *dispensatio*.

The term *distinctio* suggests that there are discernable differences between two entities in relation (i.e. realities) that consequently form the basis for otherness or alterity. Tertullian evidently means that the Son is another Person than the Father, being numerically differentiated from the paternal figure of the Godhead, but He is not another God in relation to the Father. At least, the Son is the same God in theory (*verbo*).

Not only does Tertullian believe that the Son is numerically alterior to the Father, however, he further believes Christ is subordinate (either in function or being) to Him. Tertullian demonstrates this point by applying Ps 8:5 to the pre-incarnate heavenly Logos:

> For the Father is the whole substance, while the Son is an outflow and assignment of the whole, as he himself professes, *Because my Father is greater than I*: and by him, it is sung in the psalm, he has also been made less, *a little on this side of the angels*. So also the Father is other than the Son as being greater than the Son, as he who begets is other than he who is begotten, as he who sends is other than he who is sent, as he who makes is other than he through whom a thing is made.[9]

Tertullian contends that the Father is the entire divine substance, the Son but an "outflow and assignment of the whole" *substantia dei*.[10] Christ is a "portion" (*portio*) or "derivation" (*derivatio*) of the entire deific reality (*tota substantia*) that Tertullian worships. Tertullian frequently employs the term *substantia* in his treatises, but what he means by the referring expression is still a source of disagreement among scholars of the rhetorician.[11] This study will not attempt to solve the conundrum introduced by the famed Carthaginian. Nonetheless, it is fitting that the present study examines his use of *substantia*. Regarding Tertullian's use of *substantia*, even Osborne laments:

> Yet Tertullian, like many others, never succeeds in defining his concept of being. A first reading of *Against Praxeas* suggests that Tertullian has not avoided a division of the divine substance, and more exact scrutiny indicates that he may not have given the Son and Spirit a totality of divine substance.[12]

Tertullian does not supply a precise definition for *substantia* in *Adversus Praxean*. Nevertheless, we do know that the apologist believes that humans are rational souls wrought out of God's substance in that the Creator who is Ultimate Rationality produced mortals in His rational image (*Adv Prax* 5). Tertullian also employs *substantia* to illustrate the relationship between the Father and the Son: "For though I make two suns, yet the sun and its beam I shall count as two objects, and two manifestations of one undivided substance, in the same sense as <I count> God and his Word, the Father and the Son" (*Adv Prax* 13). In another famous passage concerning the *Logos ensarkos*, Tertullian contends that Jesus is "in one Person God and Man."[13] That is, Christ is one Person subsisting in two substances, man and God "because neither is the Word anything else but God nor the flesh anything else but man."[14] It seems that one needs to construe these statements concerning *substantia* or κρασις in the case of the hypostatic union against the backdrop of Stoicism: "His [Tertullian's] work is shot through with philosophical arguments, mostly of Stoic origin, and some creative and acute."[15] Moreover, concerning *substantia*, Osborn informs us:

> While Tertullian may use the term for a particular thing, his more exact use points to the constitutive material of a thing. This Stoic definition is always behind the concept of God's substance and is not purely material in the commonly accepted sense of today.[16]

Along with Osborn, we too think that knowledge of Stoic metaphysics elucidates Tertullian's utilization of *substantia*.[17] This means that his usage differs somewhat from the later ecclesiastical employment of *substantia* or *essentia* both during and after the Arian Controversy, which Platonic ontological schemas more profoundly influenced.[18]

Substantia does not mean "nature" in Tertullian: it signifies discrete material particulars and may refer to the "constitutive material of a thing" or entity.[19] Tertullian reasons that substance differs from nature since "a substance is one thing, and the nature of that substance is another thing; inasmuch as the substance is the special property of one given thing, whereas the nature thereof may possibly belong to many things."[20] He then provides two practical examples in order to highlight the dissimilarity between substance and nature.

The stoically influenced apologist observes that a piece of stone and a piece of iron are two distinct substances; nevertheless, the quality of hardness inhering in both differentiable substances constitutes the common nature of both *substantiae*. While hardness unites the particulars, however, the substances themselves (stone and rock) are two disparate concreta or distinct metaphysical entities. The same principle applies to wool, feathers, and the quality of softness. Wool and feathers are substances for Tertullian. He thinks that softness is the nature (*natura*) that obtains between the two particulars (*substantiae*), however.

Tertullian demonstrates how he employs *substantia* to delineate particulars, when he contends that the Father and the Son are comparable to the sun and its beam.[21] From one perspective, the sun and its rays are identical. This is especially the case when we consider the sun as one undivided substance. When a beam is considered in isolation from the sun though, it is possible to call a beam "the sun." Mentally, however, most humans pre-theoretically distinguish the sun from its rays. We usually recognize that the sun is not its beam and a beam is not the sun *simpliciter*. Nevertheless, there is another sense in which the sun and its beam are one; a ray of light emanating from the sun is an extension of the sun's *substantia*. Tertullian applies this same principle to God and His Son.[22]

The Father is comparable to the sun and Christ is akin to a ray of light going forth from the sun. As such, Christ is an extension, prolation, and manifestation of deity. He shares in the "one undivided substance" of the Father, who is the fullness of divinity. When Tertullian therefore writes that the Father is *tota substantia*, he evidently means that in the strictest sense, the Father is God. Other divine beings such as the Son only possess a relative type of divinity in a derivative or inferior sense: "The Father is the whole substance, while the Son is only a derivation who participates in the divine substance in a lesser degree than the Father."[23] The Father is thus greater than the Son is—both in the economy (*oikonomia*) and immanently (*quoad se*). O'Collins suggests that Tertullian's belief that the Father is the *tota substantia* of the Godhead could "readily imply that the Son does not enjoy the fullness of divinity."[24] Tertullian's language regarding the Son's divine status must accordingly be nuanced.

There are two salient points that we need to underscore at this point. First, we have seen how Tertullian makes it clear that the Father is the whole substance of the Godhead, the Son but a derivation and part of the whole. This affirmation about the Father and His Son applies to the pre-incarnate Logos who becomes a Son to God before and for the purpose of creation.[25] *Adv Prax* 9 indicates that Christ in his *Präexistenz* is the subject of discussion, and not Discourse enfleshed. Tertullian reasons:

> So also the Father is other than the Son as being greater than the Son, as he who sends is other than he who is sent, as he who begets is other than he who is begotten, as he who makes is other than he through whom a thing is made.[26]

By articulating his Christology in these terms, Tertullian provides the figurative ground (*Grund*) for introducing the notion of subordination and otherness into the economic Trinity. The economy is not utterly reducible to the *incarnatio Christi*, however. Ergo, while Tertullian invokes Jn 14:28 in *Adv Prax* 9, he does so to demonstrate how the Son relates to the Father in the Godhead apart from His *Menschwerdung*. Tertullian also appeals to Ps 8:5 which delineates the temporary minoration of God's Son prior to His becoming flesh.

A second point we want to draw attention to is that Tertullian's exegesis of Ps 8:5 in *Adv Prax* 9 reveals that he believes God the Father made the pre-existent Son lower than the angels for a time, by generating Him antecedent to creation. Hence, this study urges that the Son became lower than the angels before He assumed flesh. This means that Tertullian evidently affirms the superiority of the Father over against the Son independently of the Son's human state. If Tertullian does indeed posit this view, as this investigation argues, one wonders how he can concomitantly affirm the absolute (i.e. unqualified) deity of the Son. How can one who is fully God be lower than the angels, if He does not possess a human οθσια? How can Tertullian consistently hold that the Son is truly God (*vere deus*), if he believes that Christ is only a "portion" of the entire divine substance with respect to the Godhead?

To address these questions, one might reason that Tertullian thinks the Son decided to submit Himself eternally to the Father's omnipotent Will without relinquishing His absolute deity. Therefore, although the Son had a beginning and was not always such according to Tertullian, He is fully God since he originates from the Father's very substance.[27] Alternatively, Tertullian might also think the Son was lower than the angels in his pre-existence because He came to be in a position wherein He could add humanity to His spiritual nature in preparation for being a human in the firsy century. Despite the two suggestion essayed here, we submit that it is quite possible that the most convincing explanation to the seeming quandary discussed in this paragraph is provided in *Adv Marc* 2.27, a text that we analyzed above:

> He is the Son of the Creator, his Word whom by bringing him forth from himself he caused to be his Son. From then onwards he put him in authority over his whole design and purpose, reducing him a little below the angels, as it is written in David.

Based on this passage, we can tentatively conclude that Tertullian believes the Son of God was made lower than the angels by means of His temporal pre-enfleshed generation. The Son consequently experiences a "lessening" when God brings Him forth ante creation as *filius qua filius*.[28] From henceforth, the Son as such becomes lower than the angels. Additionally, the angelophanies in the OT serve as further evidence that the Son's temporal minoration occurred before His Incarnation. We will now consider Tertullian's treatment of such angelophanies as he delineates them in *Adv Prax* 16.

B. ADVERSUS PRAXEAN 16

Tertullian relates that the Son is the intermediate agent of every divine judicial act described in the OT. The pre-existent Son confounded the languages at Babel, brought forth the deluge of waters upon the incorrigible generation of Noah's day, and rained down fire and brimstone on the two cities of Sodom and Gommorah for their fragrant acts of disobedience.[29] Furthermore, "He it always was who came down to converse with men, from Adam even to the patriarchs and prophets, always from the beginning preparing beforehand in dream and in a mirror and in an enigma that course which He was going to follow out to the end."[30]

Tertullian's position with respect to the angelophanies of Christ is admittedly inconsistent. In certain passages, he avers that the Father is transcendent and perpetually invisible to eyes that belong to bodies constituted of flesh. The Father, Tertullian insists, is wholly incapable of condescending in order to manifest Himself perceptibly to carnal (i.e. physical or earthly) somatic beings.[31] The pre-incarnate Son, on the other hand, is able to assume flesh and visibly appear to rational creaturely essences. He literally takes on a human corpus (somewhat) and converses with the ancient Hebrew patriarchs and prophets in preparation for His first century Incarnation, Tertullian claims, in *Adv Prax* 14. In *De Carne* 6, we also read:

> But the Lord Himself at that very time appeared to Abraham among those angels without being born, and yet in the flesh without doubt, in virtue of the before-mentioned diversity of cause. You, however, cannot admit this, since you do not receive that Christ, who was even then rehearsing how to converse with, and liberate, and judge the human race, in the habit of a flesh which as yet was not born, because it did not yet mean to die until both its nativity and mortality were previously (by prophecy) announced.

In what is evidently a metanoian moment, however, the apologist seems to adjust his stance in *Adv Prax* 16. There we witness Tertullian having difficulty believing that the Son really assumed a body of flesh when he exhibited himself to the Hebrew patriarchs and prophets in angelophanies.[32] As an alternative, he proposes that the Angelomorphic Son actually appeared "in dream and in a mirror and in an enigma that course which he was going to follow out to the end."[33] Evans observes:

> Tertullian therefore in the present passage [*Adv Prax* 16], while retaining the traditional theory that the theophanies were appearances of the Son, denies their substantive reality and suggests that they were no more than visions and dreams, "as in a glass darkly" and will have it that in his own Person the Son was not seen until the Incarnation.[34]

There is clearly evidence of a dialectical tension in Tertullian's thought regarding the Father's relationship with the Son. If he holds that God the Father is the invisible or hidden divinity while the Logos is the visible and revealed aspect of God, his views are reminiscent of Gnosticism and they border on inadvertently dividing the divine substance the apologist hitherto affirms the unity of in *Adversus Praxean*.[35] To ameliorate the apparent tension, Tertullian declares that the Father made the Son lower than the angels for a time. In this way, Christ was able to converse with men through various divine media in order that He might learn how to subsist as a man through intercourse with humankind. Hence, the Son's pre-incarnate angelophanic activity supposedly explains God's *prima facie* nescience in the OT. Such angelophanies were precursors of the Messiah's enfleshed existential state. The Son's OT minoration further serves as evidence of His alterity vis-à-vis the Father. Espousing this notion allows Tertullian to posit a subordinate of status and possibly being for the pre-existent Christ in relation to the entire divine substance. The Son's assumption of a human body and passions (i.e. emotions) before He became fully human (*vere homo*) also achieved another divine intention. It served as tangible evidence that passions or psychical affections "befitted the Son, who was also going to undergo human passions, both thirst and hunger and tears and nativity itself and death itself, for this purpose made by the Father *a little lower than the angels*."[36]

As this section of the study shows, a second way in which Tertullian applies Ps 8:5 to the Son in *Adversus Praxean* is with reference to His angelophanic appearances recorded in the OT. We will now examine Tertullian's third exegetical approach to Ps 8:5 to discern how he links the Son's Incarnation with the well-known psalm.

C. ADVERSUS PRAXEAN 23

Undoubtedly, Tertullian's most common exegetical approach is to relate Ps 8:5 to the *incarnatio Christi*. One encounters this usage in *Adv Prax* 23:

> And thither also the Son looked up and prayed and made request of the Father-where also he taught us to lift ourselves up and pray, *Our Father which art in heaven*—though he is also everywhere. This the Father would have for his abode: *The heaven, he says, is my throne*. From this also he made the Son a little less than the angels by sending him down to earth, yet with the intention of crowning him with glory and honour by taking him back into heaven. This he was already granting him when he said, *I have both glorified it and will glorify it*.

The *Logos ensarkos* is provisionally inferior to the angels. Of course, His temporary earthly minoration culminates in His everlasting celestial glorification. Nevertheless, the subordinate status of Christ actually begins before and in anticipation of His assumed humanity, according to Tertullian's account. In fact, its starting point is at the very commencement of God's creative activity (*Adv Marc* 2.27), the *initus creationis*. In this way, the Logos who becomes God's Son is made lower than the angels by virtue of His temporal generation (*Adv Herm* 3.18). As noted hitherto, *Adv Prax* 9 seems to bear this point out as well. However, there are some objections to the interpretation essayed in this study that we need to consider closely.

Roy Kearsley has argued that Tertullian (in *Adv Prax* 9) restricts the application of Ps 8:5 to the function of the Logos in God's redemptive historical dealings (*Heilsgeschichte*). More specifically, he claims that the verse has reference to the incarnate Son and not to Christ in His pre-existence.[37] Is it possible that a text such as *Adv Prax* 9 regarding the Son's momentary state of inferiority in relation to the angels does not refer to His pre-existent state but only possesses significance in accordance with His assumption of humanity? We will now examine Kearsley's line of argumentation and offer a critical assessment of it.

D. KEARSLEY AND TERTULLIAN'S INTERPRETATION OF PS 8:5 IN ADV PRAX 9

Roy Kearsley has written a groundbreaking and informative work setting forth Tertullian's theology of divine power. He contends that the substance (*substantia*) spoken of in *Adv Prax* 9 is transmitted from the Father to the Son without division or separation. God the Father communicates the "whole substance of the Deity" to the Son without the latter undergoing any diminution with respect to the one divine Godhead.[38] Additionally, Kearsley contends that *substantia* may denote "a substratum" (reality) indigenous to the three opposed relations that putatively constitute the Trinity, even though the Father is evidently the total substance of the Godhead.[39] He then cites the significant formula *pater enim tota substantia est, filius vero derivatio totius et portio* that appears to define the relationship between the Father and one of His lesser prolations.[40] With regard to the Son's derivation (*derivatio*) from the Father, Kearsley notes: "Evans concludes that a certain lessening of the Son in his divine being occurs here."[41] He seems reluctant, however, to concur with Evans in this respect and discreetly warns that one should avoid interpreting Tertullian in a crude materialistic manner.

Kearsley also refuses to concede that Tertullian predicates a "minor portion" (the Son) being "cut off from the larger and superior mass called the Father."[42] He recommends stressing *derivatio* more so than *portio* since he thinks that *portio* does not merely signify "portion" in *Adv Prax* 9. He apparently bases this intepretation on Tertullian's employment of *prolatio* in *Adv Prax* 14, to depict the relationship between the Father and the Son. Kearsley, based on this passage, infers that we should equate *prolatio* with *portio* and not with *pars*.[43]

In addition to the foregoing, Kearsley suggests that Jn 14:28, a text that Tertullian cites in *Adv Prax* 9 and 14, pertains to God's historical redemptive scheme or *oikonomia*. That is, God's *modus operandi* for effecting salvation in human history (*Heilsgeschichte*). Supposedly, Tertullian's quote from Ps 8:5 supports Kearsley's line of argumentation that the ancient song as implemented by Tertullian is not concerned with the Son's pre-cosmic generation. Rather, the locus of its referential significance is the Incarnation of the God-Man. Ergo, the Son is an "assignment of the whole" in the work of redemption: Christ is only an "assignment and outflow" (*portio et derivatio*) in His capacity as the corporeal or human Son of God, Kearsley maintains.

If his *posita* are warranted, then the thesis advanced in this study regarding the pre-existent Christ being lower than the angels since God said "*lux fiat*" appears to be in jeopardy. Before capitulating to the views espoused by Kearsley though, we shall now assess his treatment of Tertullian's concept of *substantia* in the light of *Adv Prax* 9 to ascertain its historical viability. The following assessment will review Kearsley's contentions in the order that we have outlined them.

E. CRITIQUE OF KEARSLEY'S TREATMENT

Kearsley states that both the Son and the Holy Spirit are "equal possessors" (*consortes*) of the Father's substance.[44] The Father is the whole substance while the Son is an eternal expression and outflow of the whole substance. The Persons are distinct without being separate. Finally, Kearsley maintains that Tertullian teaches each Person is fully God, co-equal in substance and co-omnipotent. He concludes: "Son and Spirit [in Tertullian's writings] possess parity in divine power because they come forth from the divine substance."[45]

> As mentioned above, it is very difficult to ascertain what Tertullian precisely means by the term *substantia*. Regardless of what the Latin expression signifies in *Adversus Praxean* or other apologetical and polemical works, it is almost certain that Tertullian does not believe the Son or Holy Spirit possess divinity in its fullness. The Father is not simply the entire divine substance; He is the plenitude of divinity, whereas the Son is but a part. Moreover, Tertullian exclaims that God has not always been a Father or a Judge since there was a time when neither sin nor the Son existed beside Him (*Adv Herm* 3.18): God became a Father. For this reason, Fortman finds Tertullian's doctrine of Christ wanting.[46] The ancient Christian rhetorician does not accept the eternal generation of the Son; yet, he articulates the point so clearly that there was never a time when God *qua* God was not.

Bernard Lonergan also points to the seemingly contradictory elements in Tertullian's Christology, noting that the Carthaginian rightly believes that the Father is not the Son nor is the Son the Father, yet he affirms that both hypostases are God. Nevertheless, Tertullian thinks that the Son is temporal while the divine Person who became *deus pater* is eternal. Moreover, he says that the Father is the whole substance of divinity, though the Son is but a *portio* and *derivatio* of the divine; he confirms that the Father commands while the Son obeys the dictates of the Father. Lastly, the Father creates while the

Son mediates. In short, Tertullian appears to gainsay the primary argument advanced in *Adversus Praxean*, Lonergan writes.[47] For, if the Son is God and God is eternal (i.e. timeless), then the Son must be eternal. Furthermore, "if the Son is God, and God is the whole divine substance, then the Son also is the whole divine substance; if the Son is God, and God commands, then the Son also commands."[48] Otherwise, Tertullian inadvertently puts forth contradictory propositions. One may proffer a solution to Lonergan's charge that Tertullian's Christology is logically inconsistent by noting that Tertullian does not think the Son is fully God. Tertullian evidently believes that the Son possesses a relative type of divinity, thereby making him dependent on the Father's absolute and unqualified ουσια.[49] Mellone thus appears to be correct when he observes that Tertullian affirms a subordination of essence for the Son.[50]

1. Kearsley's Argument in Favor of Portio

Kearsley next contends that *portio* does not simply mean "portion" in *Adv Prax* 9. By positing this thetic judgment, he is endeavoring to avoid an unsophisticated or materialistic construal of *portio* in Tertullian, although it is quite possible to understand *portio* as being equivalent to *pars* without imputing a crass or rudimentary materialistic stance to Tertullian since his employment of *portio* appears to be metaphorical.[51] Consequently, it seems apropos for Latin writers to use *portio* as a semantic equivalent for *pars*: the two terms are overlapping relations. *Portio* denotes "part, portion" in Tacitus and Pliny.[52] Augustine employs it to signify *partie*, and Tertullian utilizes it metaphorically to denote "resemblance." The term means, "part" (i.e. *soin pre'fere'* or *objet pre'fere*) in other ecclesiastical writings as well.[53] *Portio* may well signify "part" or "portion" in a tropical (non-literal) sense; it need not and probably does not mean "assignment" in *Adv Prax* 9.6. Lexical semantics not only indicate that *portio* signifies "part" or "portion," but the syntax of the passage in *Adversus Praxean* further suggests that *portio* denotes "portion" in *Adv Prax* 9.

Evans thinks that Tertullian qualifies *portio* with *totius*, thus making this construction syntactically a descriptive instead of a partitive genitive (i.e. genitive of the whole).[54] The Son is not a part, but a "purtenance of divinity," he argues.[55] Christ does not exhaust deity but is, nevertheless, fully God as "an assignment of the whole", Evans maintains.[56]

Evans cites a number of texts that appear to support understanding *portio totius* as a descriptive genitive.[57] For instance, he quotes *Adv Prax* 26.11–13, which reads: "For when he said The Spirit of God, although God is spirit, yet since he did not mention God in the nominative case he wished there to be understood an assignment of the whole which was to go to the Son's account."[58] While one could certainly read the words here in *Adversus Praxean* as a descriptive genitive, it is also possible to construe this portion of the work as a wholative genitive.[59] It is difficult to settle this issue on the basis of grammar alone. However, the manner in which Tertullian and other pre-Nicenes employ *portio* lends credence to the view that the construction, "portion of the whole" (*portio totius*) is a genitive of the whole or partitive genitive.

Two texts that suggest *portio totius* is a partitive genitive in *Adv Prax* 9 are Novatian's *De Trin* 11 ("*quoniam nec tenebit perfectam veritatem quisquis aliquam veritatis excluserit portionem*") and Tertullian's *Adv Marc* 3.6 ("*per eiusdem substantiae condicionem, cuius si plenitudo intellecta non est, multo magis portio, certe qua plenitudinis consors*").[60] In the final analysis, we must admit that certainty eludes us concerning this issue, though the pre-Nicene and classical data seem to point toward *portio totius* being a wholative genitive. Yet, Kearsley not only contends that the phrase, *portio totius*, should be translated "assignment of the whole," (a descriptive genitive), he further argues that Tertullian applies Jn 14:28 exclusively to the incarnate Son in *Adv Prax* 9. We will now critically assess Kearsley's remarks regarding Jn 14:28 in the next part of this study.

2. Kearsley's Application of John 14:28

Kearsley avers that Tertullian refers solely to the Logos ensarkos when he references Jn 14:28 in *Adv Prax* 9. The text, Kearsley declares, applies to the economy and only to the economy. However, the context of *Adv Prax* 9 indicates that Tertullian does not think that Ps 8:5 or Jn 14:28 only have the Logos *ensarkos* as their specified referent. This point seems evident from Tertullian's exegesis of Ps 8:5 in *Adv Marc* 2.27 and the ante-Nicene exegesis of Jn 14:28.

While some church fathers chose to apply Jn 14:28 exclusively to the human nature of Christ, Barrett demonstrates that this textual reading neither represents the earliest traditional way that Christians interpreted the text nor the predominant way that the pre-Nicenes exgeted the Johannine passage.[61] Most early church writers thought that Jn 14:28 was to be explained "independently of the circumstances of the incarnation."[62] Barrett's evaluation of the exegetical history of Jn 14:28 is confirmed in *Adv Prax* 14, where Tertullian unambiguously applies the Johannine passage to the Son without restricting it to the Incarnation. In *Adv Prax* 22, Tertullian refers Jn 10:30 to the heavenly Logos. Origen also thinks Jn 14:28 teaches that the Father is greater than the Son according to "their proper being and intrinsic relationship"[63] and Irenaeus seems to hold a similar doctrinal view.[64] Additionally, Tertullian believes that Jn 1:9 is a reference to the preexistent Son (*Adv Prax* 12): Christ, in His pre-existent state, is called "assistant and minister" of the Father.[65] It should therefore not come as a surprise if verses commonly interpreted as references to the human ousia of Christ in post-Nicene times, were viewed as allusions to the immanent relationship of the Father and Son by most pre-Nicenes. We therefore conclude that Tertullian follows a common pre-Nicene pattern and interprets Jn 14:28 "independently of the circumstances of the incarnation."

Now that we have assessed Kearsley's arguments, we will report the findings of this study and conclude by showing the relevance of the investigation we have undertaken. In doing so, we will further summarize the main points emphasized throughout this study.

NOTES

1. *Adv Marc* 2:27.
2. *Adv Prax* 5–11. Compare Justin's *Dialogus cum Tryphone* 62.4.
3. *De Carne* 14.
4. *Adv Prax* 9: "Hanc me regulam professum, qua inseparatos ab alterutro patrem et filium et spiritum testor, tene ubique, et ita quid quomodo dicatur agnosces. ecce enim dico alium esse patrem et alium filium et alium spiritum (male accepit idiotes quisque aut perversus hoc dictum, quasi diversitatem sonet et ex diversitate separationem protendat patris et filii et spiritus: necessitate autem hoc dico cum eundem patrem et filium et spiritum contendunt, adversus oeconomiam monarchiae adulantes) non tamen diversitate alium filium a patre sed distributione, nec divisione alium sed distinctione, quia non sit idem pater et filius, vel modulo alias ab alio."
5. Kelly, *Early Christian Doctrines*, 119.
6. *Adv Prax* 3.
7. Ibid.
8. Evans, *Adversus Praxean*, 244.
9. *Adv Prax* 9: "Pater enim tota substantia est, filius vero, derivatio totius et portio, sicut ipse profitetur, Quia pater maior me est: a quo et minoratus canitur in psalmo, Modicum quid citra angelos. sic et pater alias a filio, dum filio maior, dum alias qui generat alius qui generatur, dum alius qui mittit alius qui mittitur, dum alius qui facit alius per quem fit."
10. "It must, certainly, be admitted that Tertullian cannot escape the charge of subordinationism. He bluntly calls the Father the whole divine substance, and the Son a part of it" (Morgan, *The Importance of Tertullian*, 264–265). Morgan also notes that Tertullian illustrates the relationship between the Father and the Son by appealing to the sun, the "parent mass" which has beams of light functioning as extensions of the parent mass. A beam, Morgan observes, is obviously part of the sun, these two substances being two "distinct things (*species*)." However, Tertullian's analogy suggests a subordination of essence between the Son and Father.

11. Osborn (*Tertullian*, 131) continues: "Unity was a matter of substance. God's substance might mean God himself, his mode of existence, his rank or character, his divinity or eternity. Another meaning suggests 'the unique stuff which is, or composes, the divine corpus, and which Tertullian denotes spiritus.'" See also Stead "Divine Substance in Tertullian," *JTS* NS 14 (1963) 46–66. For further study, consult Tertullian's *Adv Prax* 31.1; *Adv Herm* 3; *Apol* 21. Tertullian posits a notion of nonmaterial matter (*stoffloses Stoff*), according to Osborn, *Tertullian*, 132.

12. Ibid.

13. *Adv Prax* 27.

14. Ibid. The Son is an effluence of the divine substance according to Tertullian's *Apology* 21.

15. Hall, *Doctrine and Practice*, 69.

16. Osborn, *Tertullian*, 131.

17. The four Stoic categories are substance, quality, disposition and relative disposition (Osborn, *Tertullian*, 125–126). Stoic metaphysics deals with "individually qualified entities." See appendix IV.

18. See Brox

19. Ibid. 131. Cf. Hall, *Doctrine and Practice*, 72. He thinks that *substantia* can denote "a being," especially when God is the referent of the term.

20. *De Anima* 32.

21. *Adv Prax* 13.

22. Ibid.

23. J. L. Neve and Otto W. Heick, *A History of Christian Thought* (Philadelphia: Fortress Press, 1965–1966), 108.

24. *The Tripersonal God*, 107.

25. "The Son and the Spirit are distinguished, therefore, from the Father in that they have their own subsistent being, which is not, however, based on their eternal specific individuality, but rather on their function in relation to God's creation. Tertullian does not manage to get beyond the combination of a modalism with regard to the distinctness of the individual persons and a subordinationism with regard to their existential plurality" (Daniélou, *History of Early Christian Doctrine*, 3:364).

26. *Adv Prax* 9.

27. Fortman, *Triune God*, 114–115.

28. Bethune-Baker also observes that the pre-incarnate Son is "made less" than the Father (*Adv Prax* 9). But he overlooks the fact that the preincarnate Christ is also made inferior to the angels (*Early History*, 142).

29. *Adv Prax* 16.

30. See *Adv Prax* 16.28–32: "Ipse enim et ad humana semper colloquia descendit, ab Adam usque ad patriarchas et prophetas, in visione in somnio in speculo in aenigmate ordinem suum praestruens ab initio semper quem erat persecutors in finem."

31. *Adv Prax* 14.

32. Wiles, *Making*, 125–126.

33. *Adv Prax* 16.

34. Evans, *Adversus Praxean*, 269.

35. Brown, *Heresies*, 42–60.

36. *Adv Prax* 16. Cf. *Adv Marc* 2.16.

37. Colish thinks that Tertullian teaches the consubstantiality of the Son or at least provides a basis for later thinkers to define the hypostatic union. She writes: "He wants to emphasize the consubstantiality of the Son with the Father over against heretics who reject the principle that the fullness of divinity dwells in Christ" (*The Stoic Tradition*, 2:22–23).

38. Kearsley, *Tertullian's Theology*, 122.

39. Ibid.

40. *Adv Prax* 9.34. This section of *Adversus Praxean* also contains an allusion to Jn 14:28 indicating that the Son is, in some fashion, subordinate to the Father. We will later discuss Tertullian's application of Jn 14:28.

41. Kearsley, *Tertullian's Theology*, 122.

42. Ibid.

43. Ibid. 123.

44. Ibid. 124.

45. Ibid.

46. Fortman, *Triune God*, 115.

47. For a discussion of Tertullian's efforts to remove the material principle (objective contradiction) from his thought, see Lonergan, *The Way to Nicea*, 48–49. Lonergan further explains the means employed by Tertullian and other pre-Nicenes to eradicate theological inconsistences from their respective systems. According to Lonergan, the necessary elements for resolving dialectical tension in one's system are the formal principle (i.e. the rational subject illumined by natural reason or the light of faith) and the dialectic process (i.e. the actual act itself of eliminating contradictions). Furthermore, Lonergan speaks about the "term" or the result of the dialectical process (either heresy or advance in theology as well as orthodoxy). The *terminus* of Christian dialectical movement will depend on whether natural reason is involved or reason is illumined by faith, according to Lonergan.

48. Lonergan shows further apparent logical incongruities in Tertullian's thought through the use of simple syllogisms: "if the Son is God, and God is the whole divine substance, then the Son also is the whole divine substance; if the Son is God, and God commands, then the Son also commands" (ibid. 48).

49. C. C. Richardson, *The Christianity of Ignatius of Antioch* (New York: Columbia University Press, 1935), 45.

50. Mellone, *Leaders*, 178.

51. See Bertrand de Margerie, *The Christian Trinity in History* (Still River: St. Bede, 1982), 78–81.

52. Albert Blaise, *Dictionnaire Latin-Francais Des Auteurs Chrétiens: Revu Specialement Pour le Vocabulaire Théologique* (Brepolis: de Strasbourg 1954 [1993]), 635.

53. Ibid. 635.

54. Evans, *Adversus Praxean*, 247.

55. Ibid. 246.

56. See *Adv Prax* 26; cf. Kearsley, *Tertullian's Theology*, 123.

57. Evans, *Adversus Praxean*, 246.

58. "Dicens autem, Spiritus dei, etsi spiritus dei, tamen non directo deum nominans portionem totius intellegi voluit quae cessura erat in filii nomen."

59. Compare Juvenal's *Satura* 9.128ff: "festinat enim decurrere velox flosculus angustae miseraeque breuissima uitae portio; dum bibimus, dum serta, unguenta, paellas poscimus, obrepit non intellecta senectus Satura."

60. *De Trin* 11: "because anyone who should exclude one *portion* of the truth will never hold the perfect truth." *Adv Marc* 3:6: "he is one and the same substance, with the same attributes, and if the fullness of this was beyond their understanding, so, *a fortiori*, was the derivative, seeing it is joint possessor with the fullness." Compare *De Res* 16.

61. C. K. Barrett's *Essays on John* (London: SPCK, 1982), 27. See the Tome of Leo (*Ad Flavianum, Epistola* 4) and Augustine's *Tractate on John* 78.2.

62. Barrett lists Tertullian's *Adv Prax* 9 as one example of a pre-Nicene applying Jn 14:28 to the Son independently of His incarnate state. Barrett, *Essays*, 27.

63. Ibid. 27–28.

64. Irenaeus reasons: "For if any one should inquire the reason why the Father, who has fellowship with the Son in all things, has been declared by the Lord alone to know the hour and the day [of judgment], he will find at present no more suitable, or becoming, or safe reason than this (since, indeed, the Lord is the only true Master), that we may learn through Him that the Father is above all things. For "the Father," says He, "is greater than I." The Father, therefore, has been declared by our Lord to excel with respect to knowledge; for this reason, that we, too, as long as we are connected with the scheme of things in this world, should leave perfect knowledge, and such questions [as have been mentioned], to God, and should not by any chance, while we seek to investigate the sublime nature of the Father, fall into the danger of starting the question whether there is another God above God." *Adv Haer* 2.28.3.

65. *Adv Prax* 12.

Conclusion
Findings Regarding Tertullian, Psalm 8:5 and Angelomorphic Christology

The initial goal of this study was to explore three questions dealing with Angelomorphic Christology and Ps 8:5. We will now outline three findings of this inquiry in succession.

(1) Daniélou writes that Tertullian rejects all angelopmorphic Christology. After exploring Tertullian's writings, however, we are inclined to believe that Daniélou's reading of Tertullian either must be nuanced or the noted ecclesiastical historian is employing the standard nomenclature of angelomorphic studies imprecisely. For while Tertullian is reluctant to call Christ an angel and he most certainly has a manifest "distaste" for Angelomorphic Christology, the Carthaginian does not repudiate angelomorphism *tout court*. His writings show that he believes there is a sense in which Christ is or reveals himself as an angel in enigmata, dreams and visions when the Will of God deems such angelomorphic manifestations to be appropriate. Tertullian explicitly calls Christ an angel in *De Carne* 14. Furthermore, the Christian rhetor readily makes use of angelomorphic themes. Maybe, as Stuckenbruck suggests, one should speak of Tertullian's angelophanic Christology in view of the way that he depicts Christ as the angel of the Lord (*malak YHWH*) who appeared to the Hebrew patriarchs and prophets of antiquity. At any rate, we think it is safe to submit that Tertullian does not reject all Angelomorphic Christology.

(2) More than one commentator has stated that Tertullian thinks there is an ontological divide between Christ and the holy angels of God. Daniélou appeals to *Adv Prax* 3.4-10 to buttress this contention. However, this particular section of Tertullian's work may not provide sufficient warrant for positing a categorical difference of being between Christ and the angels since the translation and textual reading of this passage is definitively uncertain. Furthermore, other

parts of Tertullian's work indicate that the angels probably share in the substance, though not the being of God.¹ If humans, as finite rational agents, share in the *substantia dei*, according to Tertullian, then should not the holy angels also partake of the Father's substance? After all, they are supposed to be superior to humankind in terms of status and ontic particularity. Additionally, Tertullian indicates that the angels administer God's *monarchia*: myriads and myriads of spirit beings attend God's throne and uphold it (Dan 7:10). They are thus officials of the esteemed divine monarchy advocated by Tertullian. This study thus concludes that Tertullian does not posit an ontological chasm vis-à-vis the angels and the two *prolationes* of the Trinity. The angels, the influential apologist from Carthage seems to argue, are 'ομοουσιον τω πατρι και υιει.

(3) The main contention of this study is that God temporarily made the Son *qua* Son lower than the angels. We base this argument primarily on two texts from Tertullian's corpus, namely, *Adv Marc* 2.27 and *Adv Prax* 9. Tertullian mainly invokes Ps 8:5 when he is referring to the Logos *ensarkos*. He further applies the text to the Son as He appears in angelophanies. However, *Adv Marc* 2.27 unambiguously declares that the pre-angelophanic and pre-enfleshed Discourse of God became lower than the angels when God generated Him before and for the purpose of creation. The basis for such a subordinate position in relation to the angels is the *perfecta nativitas sermonis*, an event that occurs prior to creation. This complete nativity of *sermo* occurs when God exclaims, fiat *lux*, at the *initus creationis* (*Adv Prax* 5-7) In this respect, Tertullian argues that the Son is both inferior to and other than the Father in *Adv Prax* 9. These comments apply to the pre-existent Christ in view of how Tertullian and other pre-Nicenes exegete Jn 14:28.

IMPLICATIONS OF THIS STUDY

Tertullian was well versed in the OT writings. Furthermore, he demonstrates a certain familiarity with various scriptural divine appellations, readily and frequently using titles contained in both the Law and the Prophets that appertain to deity. This zealous spokesman for Christianity taught that the Son is *omnipotens* or literally the self-designation (*nomen*) of the Father since Christ manifests Himself angelically in the Father's name.² Despite formulating a somewhat "high Christology" and interpreting OT references concerning YHWH as allusions to Christ, Tertullian was nevertheless careful to note that the two deific beings that he so clearly and emphatically affirms in *Adversus Praxean* are clearly not equal in eternity, power or divinity. According to Tertullian's theology, the divinity of the second Lord (i.e. the Son) is relative, that is, the Son's deity is not absolute since his deity completely dependent for its existence on the Father's Godhood. Furthermore, the second Lord is evidently subordinate to the Father with respect to His *essentia* even before He assumes humanity. Moreover, Tertullian also believes that the Son *qua* Son is inferior to the angels prior to His enfleshment. This point is clearly brought out in Adv Marc 2.27; Adv 9.

Tertullian also thinks that the glorious and designated Lord or Son of God is not an eternal divine *persona*. Rather, the apologist believes that the *ratio dei* becomes a Son or personal agent *in tempo* when God verbally expresses His own immanent Logos. All of the forgoing means that there is no doubt a marked ontological disparity between the two Lords toward whom Tertullian displays reverence. Wilken's observation comes to mind, when he writes that the pre-Nicenes thought Christ was God, in some sense, but they did not believe He was "fully God":

> During these years [the first three centuries of Christianity's existence], most Christians vaguely thought of Jesus as God; yet they did not actually think of him in the same way as they thought of God the Father. They seldom addressed prayers to him, and thought of him somehow as second to God—divine, yes, but not fully God.[3]

Two fundamental tenets of Christianity are: (1) God is one divine being; (2) God has revealed Himself through Jesus Christ at the fullness of time (Gal 4:4). In this regard, Richardson points out that the basis of Christian belief is God's unicity and the divine self-disclosure "in Jesus Christ."[4] He then adds:

> When the early Christians found it necessary to consider the implications of this conviction they did not find it difficult to suppose that the God *qui est super omnia* allowed his monarchy to be administered by the Son, who was dependent upon Him for immortality and a relative divinity.[5]

At this point, Richardson unequivocally has Tertullian in mind. He explictly writes: "This is the basis of the argument of Tertullian against Praxeas. The popular idea of the relative divinity of the 'created gods' can be found in Plato (Tim. 41), and, in Stoicism, man is 'o θεος because he possesses reason, or part of the essence of the Godhead."[6]

The conclusion that we thus draw from the research undertaken here is that Tertullian's doctrine of Christ does not escape a certain subordination of essence. In *Adversus Praxean*, the accomplished *rhetor* presents Christ as a supernatural being, who only possesses a relative form of divinity. Tertullian distinctly qualifies the Son's deity, carefully distinguishing Him (ontologically) from the Father, "who is over all" (*qui est super omnia*). There may even be a sense in which the pre-existent Christ could be spoken of as a "created god" in view of Tertullian's leanings towards Stoicism and his detailed exegesis of Prov 8:22-31, which speaks of the created Wisdom of God. But Tertullian never explicitly affirms that the Son was created *ex nihilo*.

In conclusion, we seem to be justified in saying that while his particular form of Christian teaching did not permanently influence the Christian Church, the theological language that Tertullian utilized to delineate the putative relationship between the three persons of the Trinity (*tres personae trinitatis*) did have a lasting effect on the subsequent formulation of the Trinity doctrine and the church's theological doctrine of Christ. With these developments in mind, Quasten notes: "It is in the doctrine of the Trinity and the intimately connected Christology that Tertullian made the greatest contribution to theology".[7] Consequently, Milman does not speak hyperbolically, when he notes that Tertullian was the first Latin writer to gain a public hearing and, in view of his activities, one can thus conclude: "Africa, not Rome, gave birth to Latin Christianity."[8]

NOTES

1. D. S. Russell. *The Method and Message of Jewish Aocalyptic* (Philadelphia: Westminster Press, 1964), 235.
2. See Tertullian's *De Oratio* 1.
3. Wilken, *Christian Beginnings*, 179.
4. Richardson, *Ignatius of Antioch*, 44.
5. Ibid. 44-45.
6. Ibid. 98.
7. *Patrology*, 324. While I basically concur with the analysis found in Quasten's *Patrology*, I also think that it is important to make a distinction between Tertullian's contribution to Trinitarian *language* and his contribution to the ontological dogma itself. One thus seems justified in concluding that Tertullian is a long way from Nicaea in his thinking and treatment of the Trinity, a point apparently admitted by Quasten himself (326). We do well, therefore, to avoid retrojecting Nicaean language or post-Nicene ontological categories back onto Tertullian's *Adversus Praxean*. Contra Osborn, Tertullian does not believe that the "economic Trinity is the immanent Trinity" (a phrase popularized by Karl Rahner) and vice versa (see Osborn, *Tertullian*, 121). Harnack appears to be correct when he limits Tertullian's "Trinity" to God's economy or *Heilsgeschichte*.
8. Henry Milman, *History of Latin Christianity: Including that of the Popes to the Pontificate of Nicolas V*, 8 vols. (New York: W. J. Widdleton, 1870), 1:56-59.

Appendix

I. PERSONA AND TERTULLIAN

What does Tertullian intend to say when he categorizes the three hypostases, which presumably constitute the Trinity, as *personae*? Does he thereby impute consciousness to each divine Person?

Grillmeier examines Tertullian's use of the Latin signifier and remarks that he rarely utilizes *persona* to mean, "mask" or "theatre role."[1] Alternatively, there are about thirty occurrences of the term in Tertullian's writings that simply appear to denote "person." Grillmeier thus suggests that the ardent Latin pre-Nicene assigns individuality or concreteness to the expression at times. Tertullian may also perceive a conceptual nexus between *persona* and *substantia* in *Adversus Praxean*, but Grillmeier points out that he does not develop his treatment of this *terminus technicus* beyond the denotation or extension, "concrete presentation." *Persona* is therefore "ultimate individualization," for Tertullian.[2] He emphatically rejects the Modalist understanding of the three divine persons as successive temporary modes of being.

We are not sure if Tertullian was the first theologian to use *persona* as a descriptive term for the Father, Son or Holy Spirit. He certainly brought it to the fore by attributing a number of different senses (*Sinnen*) to the word, however. Fortman notes that in Tertullian's literary corpus, *persona* signifies "mask," "face," and is "in a sense equivalent to *homo* or *vir*." It further connotes "the concrete presentation of an individual as such."[3] Yet, Fortman points out that "the idea of self-consciousness" is not prominent in Tertullian's usage of the word.[4] The Carthaginian rhetorician evidently does not impute consciousness, at least not clearly or explicitly, to the three Persons of the Trinity. This caveat from O'Collins seems prudent: "At the same time, one must obviously beware of interpreting Tertullian in the light of later, especially modern, theories of personhood, which expounds persons as conscious selves and autonomous subjects."[5] On the other hand, we must admit that Tertullian's "Trinitarian" vocabulary presaged the terminology adopted from Nicea onward.[6]

II. SUBSTANTIA AND TERTULLIAN

Bethune-Baker maintains that Tertullian may posit a juristic denotation for substance ala Harnack, although this can hardly be what Tertullian means, in view of what he writes in *De Anima* 32 and *Adv Herm* 3. Bethune-Baker rightly notes that Tertullian uses *substantia* to signify "a particular form of existence" though he still curiously seems to argue in favor of the juristic understanding of substance in Tertullian.[7]

Substance and nature are two distinct modalities in Tertullian.[8] For example, stone and iron are two divergent substances (*substantiae*), but they share the common nature of hardness. Substance demarcates stone and iron as ontic particulars; the nature of firmness unites these particulars.[9] Bethune-Baker thus argues that substance can never mean "nature" in Tertullian.[10] Substance as it pertains to the Father, he argues, can also function as an "exegetical periphrasis" for the Father Himself. That is, as a delineation of "His own being" in view of *Adv Prax* 8.[11] Conversely, Grillmeier thinks that "By the substance of God, Tertullian understands a light, fine, invisible matter which while being a unity is differentiated within itself."[12] Father, Son and Holy Spirit therefore constitute the "one total reality of God."[13]

Blaise[14] supplies the following definitions for *substantia*: substance, matière (*Adv Prax* 14), existence (*vie*), ousia or realité (*Adv Prax* 7), être (*Adv Prax* 26); essence, nature, qualité (*Adv Prax* 16), personne, hypostasis.[15] Coupled with the aforesaid observations in this Appendix, there is ample evidence that Olson's suggestion regarding *substantia* in Tertullian's *Adversus Praxean* designating "that fundamental ontological being-ness that makes something what it is" (i.e. the unchanging and perpetual nature of an entity) does not seem to be a plausible reading of Tertullian's theory of divine substance.[16] More than likely, *substantia* in Tertullian (when applied to God) is not what Aristotle calls, secondary substance (*substantia secunda*), but primary substance (*substantia prima*). Ergo, while one may not be able to settle with objective certainty what Tertullian meant by *substantia*, we can confidently argue that Stoicism surely shaped his theory of being and doctrine of Christ.

III. SOPHIA AND ANGELOMORPHIC CHRISTOLOGY IN ADVERSUS PRAXEAN

Tertullian follows his theological predecessors in that he conceives of *Sophia* in terms of an impersonal attribute of God that is not an eternal hypostasis.[17] While Gieschen thinks that Prov 8:22–31 portrays *Sophia* as: "an hypostasis, an aspect of God that has a degree of independent personhood" or that she (grammatically speaking) is the protological "master craftsman" of *YHWH* "beside" *ha Elohim* and in His presence — Tertullian maintains that *Sophia* is a divine attribute God uses to produce the cosmos.[18] When the Most High God speaks the momentous words, "*fiat lux*," *Sophia* then becomes fully personalized and God makes *Sophia* (i.e. Wisdom) His Son. Can one legitimately speak of Wisdom's generation, as delineated by Tertullian, a creative act, however?

Gieschen proposes that the MT language of Prov 8:22 (*qanah*) actually suggests a procreative motif. He thinks that one should distinguish this particular usage of *qanah* in the MT from the Greek *ektisen* in the LXX.[19] The writer of Prov 8:22–31 (MT) supposedly depicts Wisdom as a "begotten" divine agent rather than a deific attribute: "some depictions of Wisdom go beyond the bounds of literary personification and present her as an hypostatized aspect of God."[20] Gieschen also argues that Angelomorphic motifs significantly inform a number of Wisdom traditions: "some Wisdom traditions are dependent upon and were shaped by Angelomorphic traditions"[21] James Dunn, on the other hand, insists there is no clear sign that Wisdom language goes beyond "vivid personification" in Proverbs, Sirach or any other sapiential writings.[22] The most important consideration in the present study is how Tertullian conceived Wisdom-Sophia.

When critically assessing the Arian Controversy, Wiles submits that according to the language of Scripture: "Wisdom derives its being from God, and the languages of creation and begetting are alternative designations for the same reality."[23] The two expressions actually appear to be interchanged in Isa 1:2; Deut 32:18 and Job 38:28. "Create" is accordingly a verb that semantically overlaps with the word "beget" in Scripture with the former *verbum* connoting "the unique and intimate nature of this primary act of creation."[24] Eusebius of Nicomedia reasoned in this way, and the previously mentioned Bible texts might uphold his interpretation.[25]

Werner notes that although Tertullian opposed "Angel-Christology" he did not generally dispute the reputed Christological tradition that had obtained two centuries earlier.[26] He contends that Tertullian referred to the creation of the Son in Prov 8:22–25: "Tertullian could even maintain, quite impartially, that there was no essential difference between '*natum*' and '*factum*'. Thus the creation of Logos-Christ found expression in a twofold manner."[27] Nicea later rejected such language for the *generatio filii* and even Tertullian does not explicitly say the Son came forth *ex nihilo* since he thought of Christ as an extension of divine *spiritus*.

IV. STOICISM AND SUBSTANCE

The philosophical basis for Tertullian's notion of substance is the Stoic theory of ultimate reality or being qua being. The four categories (κατηγοριαι) or predicates of Stoic metaphysics are as follows: substance, quality, disposition and relative position.[28]

Arnold explains that the Stoics considered both substance (i.e. the substrate or underlying reality) and quality to be corporeal.[29] The two categories are essentially two aspects of the same reality in Stoicism. We might then say that there is only a formal distinction (*distinctio formalis*) between the two Stoic metaphysical classifications of substance and quality.[30] Since substance (το ποιον υποκειμενον) implies existence, however, the Stoics were able to prescind from quality at times and exclusively consider the ontological primary substance or subject.[31]

The predications that the Stoics call "quality" (το ποιον, *qualitatis*) determine substance, making it entity *x* or *y*.[32] Examples of *qualitas* are sweetness, redness, hardness, softness or roundness.[33] These predicates, say the Stoics, are also corpora. Nevertheless, they cannot truly exist independently of substance. Therefore, they are corporeal realities in a secondary sense.[34] Based on the theory of universal corporeity, the Stoics accordingly define qualitative causality in terms of motive rarefaction or a decrease in density and pressure.

Disposition (πως εχοντα, *res quodammodo se habens*) is associated with sumptwmata (i.e. accidents) such as sleeping, standing, walking or running.[35] An accident, in Aristotelian and Stoic terms, is a mode of being that can only exist in another being, "as a modification or attribute of a substance" or thing.[36] It is thus non-essential or non-substantial.[37] Ergo, we may alternately describe the self-same entity as sitting, standing, walking or running. These activities are not essential properties of a substance, but accidents. The Stoics thus classify such activities as συμπτωματα.

We can illustrate relative disposition (προς τι πως εχον) or "relative accidental constitution" by pointing to right and left hand oppositions (i.e. relations) such as father and son or husband and wife, with each relation being dependent on its corresponding disposition. Slave and master or king and subject are also examples of relative dispositions.[38] Properties possessed in relation to external objects are rooted in the notion of *corpus* for the Stoics. Understanding Stoic metaphysics elucidates Tertullian's use of the term *substantia*. In the manner of the Stoics, he too emphasizes universal corporeity and stresses particulars over against Aristotelian secondary substances.[39] However, Tertullian does not uncritically adhere to the Stoic theory of ultimate reality. There are points at which he censures and even parts ways with it.

V. CARTHAGE AND CHRISTIANITY

The Libyans inhabited North Africa when the Phoenicians arrived there.[40] The Phoenicians eventually settled in Tunisia, a luxuriant area with two vast rivers named Miliana and Medjerda. The traditional date for the founding of Carthage north of Medjerda is 1101 BCE.[41] Subsequently, Punic Carthage became a nautical force that waged war with the Greeks. This area of North Africa began to expand in the fifth century, but after the three momentous Punic wars, it fell to Rome's Scipio Africanus in 146 BCE. The Romans then commandeered the territory of Carthage—distributing it as they willed.

Although Rome conquered Carthage and converted it into a province, Carthage "became the seat of the provincial governor and thus the administrative centre of this new province."[42] But the Romans granted the city exemption from taxation, so that Carthage enjoyed a privileged state of *immunitas*. Consequently, the city thrived economically, being as prosperous as "any city in Libya."[43] Tertullian, using characteristic hyperbole implied that Carthage was primarily composed of Christians in his day. At the very least, it seems that we may infer there was a burgeoning Christian community at Carthage in his day.[44] Actually, Christians were no doubt active in Carthage around 150 CE and even before that time. It seems that Christianity arrived in Carthage from the East.[45]

Regardless of how Christianity originated in Carthage, the historical starting point for the Christian religion in North Africa was the martyrdom of a few Christians at Scilli in 180 CE.[46] The martyrdom of this small group of Christians (seven men and five women), who refused to offer sacrifices to gods other than the Christian deity or swear to the "genius" of the Rome's Emperor,[47] adumbrated developments that would later transpire as Christianity continued to expand throughout North Africa.[48]

VI. TERTULLIAN AND THE REGULA FIDEI

N. T. Wright points out that the Latin term for "creed" (*symbolum*) is not fortuitous, but was deliberately chosen for semiotic reasons.[49] He reports that the first Christian statements of belief functioned as definitive religious symbols, identifying the early *communitas Christi* as worshipers of the one God revealed through Christ Jesus. Consequently, the early creeds point to a "community seeking definition."[50] That is why these symbols do not stress verbatim phrases or abstract theological formulations. They function as ecclesiastical markers (i.e. signs) nourished in a liturgical context shaped by the ancient Christian *ecclesia*.[51] This detail accounts for the different variations of the *regula fidei*. Below, we provide Tertullian's wording of the "rule of faith" so that the reader may see both the complementary ideas expressed in the *regula* that Tertullian outlines as well as the disparate notions articulated in two different literary contexts:

> Now, with regard to this rule of faith—that we may from this point acknowledge what it is which we defend—it is, you must know, that which prescribes the belief that there is one only God, and that He is none other than the Creator of the world, who produced all things out of nothing through His own Word, first of all sent forth; that this Word is called His Son, *and*, under the name of God, was seen "in diverse manners" by the patriarchs, heard at all times in the prophets, at last brought down by the Spirit and Power of the Father into the Virgin Mary, was made flesh in her womb, and, being born of her, went forth as Jesus Christ; thenceforth He preached the new law and the new promise of the kingdom of heaven, worked miracles; having been crucified, He rose again the third day; (then) having ascended into the heavens, He sat at the right hand of the Father; sent instead of Himself the Power of the Holy Ghost to lead such as believe; will come with glory to take the saints to the enjoyment of everlasting life and of the heavenly promises, and to condemn the wicked to everlasting fire, after the resurrection of both these classes shall have happened, together with the restoration of their flesh. This rule, as it will be proved, was taught by Christ, and raises amongst ourselves no other questions than those which heresies introduce, and which make men heretics. (*De Praescr Haer* 13.1–5)[52]

Notice the different emphases in the following text:

> The rule of faith, indeed, is altogether one, alone immoveable and irreformable; the rule, to wit, of believing in one only God omnipotent, the Creator of the universe, and His Son Jesus Christ, born of the Virgin Mary, crucified under Pontius Pilate, raised again the third day from the dead, received in the heavens, sitting now at the right (hand) of the Father, destined to come to judge quick and dead through the resurrection of the flesh as well (as of the spirit). (*De Vir Vel* 1.3)[53]

Bray points out that the *regula fidei* recorded in *De Praescriptione* is generally "more detailed, except, interestingly enough, in the clauses which deal with the crucifixion and the resurrection."[54]

VII. CONSORS

Consors may denote one who shares an inheritance; it can also signify a partner, colleague, or sharer (e.g. a brother, sister, wife) in other contexts.[55] The term further delineates the partaking of property in common. Latin writers employ the word to describe common heirs and the act of dividing something with one; having an equal share or partaking of a particular substance. *Consors* is also used of a partner or of subjects that share the same condition.[56] Suetonius utilizes the term to depict colleagues in power.[57]

VIII. OMNIPOTENCE OF CHRIST IN TERTULLIAN

Contra Kearsley, it seems that Tertullian believes the Son of God is Omnipotent in a qualified sense.[58] Tertullian reasons that "the Father's name is God Almighty, the Most High, the Lord of hosts, the King of Israel, I am."[59] Nevertheless, these names also apply to the Son. The Scriptures attribute divine titles to Him insofar as Christ became man, "and in these [names] always acted, and thus in himself manifested them to men."[60]

One name that the Son makes known and functions as the representative for, is God Almighty. The Son is only Omnipotent in a limited sense, however. Tertullian explains the Son's omnipotence by appealing to Mt 28:18 and Acts 2:33. The Matthean text shows that Christ apparently received His omnipotence after God raised Him from the dead. The Synoptic account significantly declares that God vouchsafed such power to Him. In Acts 2:33, the apostle Peter proclaims that God has seated Christ at His right hand. Thus, the Father has subjected all things to the Son. He is accordingly Almighty in a qualified sense.

On the other hand, Kearsley argues that the Son's omnipotence is not accidental since the quality of almightiness "belongs to the Son on account of both substance *and* economy.[61] He bases this conclusion in part on the fact that Christ by virtue of his sonship and status, as *Logos tou theou* is *omnipotens*. Admittedly, Tertullian does attribute almightiness to the Word as such, though it appears the Son *qua* Son only possesses omnipotence derivatively.

NOTES

1. Grillmeier, *Christ in Christian Tradition*, 126–127. Cf. *De Spec* 22.
2. Kelly writes that *persona* came to denote "individual" as it eventually developed from its signification "mask." Tertullian may use the term to connote the "concrete presentation of an individual as such" (*Early Christian Doctrines*, 115).

3. Fortman, *Triune God*, 113.
4. Kelly, *History of Early Doctrine*, 115.
5. O'Collins, *Tripersonal God*, 105.
6. Ibid.
7. Bethune-Baker, *Early History*, 140.
8. *De Anima* 32.
9. Bethune-Baker, *Early History*, 140–141.

10. Ibid. 141. Prestige further observes: "It may be argued that to Tertullian *substantia* did not exclude the notion of secondary substance," see *Patristic Thought*, 220. Prestige further notes that *substantia* in Tertullian refers to particulars, but *natura* may be a common feature that obtains between disparate objects. Cattle thus resemble mankind in nature but not substance. Substance is "individualised in a particular instance."

11. Bethune-Baker, *Early History*, 141. See *Adv Prax* 4 where *substantia* could have this sense.

12. Grillmeier, *Christ in Christian Tradition*, 142.
13. Ibid.
14. *Dictionnaire*, 786–787.
15. See Augustine of Hippo's *De Trin* 5.8.10.
16. Olson, *Story of Christian Theology*, 96.

17. That Tertullian thinks of *Sophia* as a divine attribute is evident from his exegesis of Prov 8:22–31 in *Adv Herm* 20.1: "When Wisdom, however, was referred to, it was quite right to say, in the beginning. For it was in Wisdom that He made all things at first, because by meditating and arranging His plans therein, He had in fact already done (the work of creation); and if He had even intended to create out of matter, He would yet have effected His creation when He previously meditated on it and arranged it in His Wisdom, since It was in fact the beginning of His ways: this meditation and arrangement being the primal operation of Wisdom, opening as it does the way to the works by the act of meditation and thought."

18. Gieschen, *Angelomorphic Christology*, 90–91.

κυριος εκτισεν με αρχν οδων αμτοῦ ει εργα αμτους προ του αιωνος ετηεμελιωσεν με εν αρχ‘η προ του την γην ποπιησαι και προ του τας αβουσσους ποιησαι προ του προελθειν τας

πηγας τφν ὑδατων προ του ὀρη εδρασθηναι προ δε παντων βουνων γεννα με κυριος εποισεν

χωρας και ἀοικητους και ακρα δι κου μενα της ὑπ' ουρανον (Prov 8:22–26 LXX, Rahlfs). Vg reads: "Dominus possedit me initium viarum suarum antequam quicquam faceret a principio ab aeterno ordita sum et ex antiquis antequam terra fieret necdum erant abyssi et ego iam concepta eram necdum fontes aquarum eruperant" (Prov 8:22–24).

19. Justin, evidently influenced by the LXX reading, uses the term "created" when delineating the generation of the Logos: "And it is written in the book of Wisdom: 'If I should tell you daily events, I would be mindful to enumerate them from the beginning. The Lord created me the beginning of His ways for His works. From everlasting He established me in the beginning, before He formed the earth, and before He

made the depths, and before the springs of waters came forth, before the mountains were settled; He begets me before all the hills.'" (*Dial* 129.3). See Hengel, *Judaism and Hellenism*, 1.162–163. Cf. Sirach 1.4, 9; 24.3; Prov 8:24–25.

20. Gieschen, *Angelomorphic Christology*, 89.
21. Ibid.
22. James D. G. Dunn, *Christology in the Making: A New Testament Inquiry into the Origins of the Doctrine of the Incarnation* (London: SCM, 1980), 170–173. See Prov 2:6; 3:19; Sirach 14.26–15.2; 42:21; Wisdom of Sol 7:22; Song of Sol 8.21–9.6.
23. Wiles, *Making*, 13.
24. Ibid.
25. Theodoret, *Church History*, 1.5.
26. Werner, *Formation*, 138–139.
27. Ibid. 139–140.
28. Arnold, *Stoicism*, 165–169. Frederick Copleston in *A History of Philosophy: Greece and Rome* (Garden City: Image Books, 1962), 130 notes that the four Stoic categories derive from the ten Aristotelian categories. He then classifies the four Stoic categories as the substrate to ὑποκείμενον, essential constitution (το ποιον ὑποκείμενον), accidental constitution (το πος εχον), and the relative accidental constitution (το προς τι πως εχον).
29. Arnold, *Stoicism*, 165.
30. See John D. Caputo's *Heidegger and Aquinas: An Essay on Overcoming Metaphysics* (New York: Fordham University Press, 1982), 68. He notes that Duns Scotus suggests that essence and existence are not two distinct realities. Scotus argues that there is only a *distinctio formalis* between existence and essence. Existence is therefore: "a formally different aspect of the selfsame reality which is both essence and existence." Hence, Scotus concludes: "Existence is real, but not a reality (a *res*)."
31. Arnold, *Stoicism*, 165.
32. Ibid.
33. Ibid. 166.
34. Rex Warner, *The Greek Philosophers* (New York: Signet, 1958), 166.
35. Arnold, *Stoicism*, 167–168. Copleston labels this category, "accidental constitution" (*A History of Philosophy*, 130).
36. Kreeft, 27.
37. Ibid.
38. Arnold, *Stoicism*, 169.
39. Lacugna makes a helpful distinction between relative states (προς τι πως εχον) and the relative *simpliciter* (προς τι). The father-son relation is a relative state or disposition, whereas bitter-sweet is a relative *simpliciter* since these two relations are capable of change and not necessarily dependent on external objects for their existence (*God for Us*, 58).
40. J. B. Rives, *Religion and Authority in Roman Carthage from Augustus to Constantine* (Oxford: Clarendon Press, 1995), 17.
41. Ibid.
42. Ibid. 22.
43. Ibid. 22–26.

44. *De Scap* 3.1; 5.2.
45. Rives, *Carthage*, 225.
46. See Milman, *Latin Christianity*, 1:56–59.
47. Metzger, *Canon*, 156–157. See Joyce E. Salisbury, *Perpetua's Passion: The Death and Memory of a Young Roman Woman* (New York: Routledge, 1997).
48. W. H. C. Frend, *The Donatist Church: A Movement of Protest in Roman North Africa* (Oxford: Clarendon Press, 1952), 87.
49. N. T. Wright, *The New Testament and the People of God* (Minneapolis: Fortress, 1992), 368.
50. Ibid.
51. Ibid.
52. "Regula est autem fidei, ut iam hinc quid defendamus profiteamur, illa scilicet qua creditur. Vnum omnino Deum esse nec alium praeter mundi conditorem qui uniuersa de nihilo produxerit per uerbum suum primo omnium emissum. Id uerbum filium eius appellatum in nomine Dei uarie uisum a patriarchis, in prophetis semper auditum, postremo delatum ex spiritu patris Dei et uirtute in uirginem Mariam, carnem factum in utero eius et ex ea natum egisse Iesum Christum. Exinde praedicasse nouam legem et nouam promissionem regni caelorum, uirtutes fecisse, cruci fixum, tertia die resurrexisse, in caelos ereptum sedisse ad dexteram patris, misisse uicariam uim spiritus sancti qui credentes agat, uenturum cum claritate ad sumendos sanctos in uitae aeternae et promissorum caelestium fructum et ad profanos adiudicandos igni perpetuo, facta utriusque partis resuscitatione cum carnis restitutione. Haec regula a Christo, ut probabitur, instituta nullas habet apud nos quaestiones nisi quas haereses inferunt et quae haereticos faciunt."
53. "Regula quidem fidei una omnino est, sola immobilis et irreformabilis, credendi scilicet in uni cum deum omnipotentem, mundi conditorem, et filium eius Iesum Christum, natum ex virgine Maria, crucifixum sub Pontio Pilato, tertia die resuscitatum a mortuis, receptum in caelis, sedentem nunc ad dexteram patris, venturum iudi care vivos et mortuos per carnis etiam resurrectionem."
54. Bray, *Holiness*, 100–101.
55. OLD 1:418.
56. Virgil, *Georgicon* 4.153.
57. *Tit* 9.
58. See Kearsley, *Tertullian's Theology*, 115.
59. *Adv Prax* 17.
60. Ibid.
61. Kearsley, *Tertullian's Theology*, 128.

Bibliography

I. TEXTS AND TRANSLATIONS

Adversus Hermogonem. Trans. E. Evans. Oxford: Clarendon Press, 1972.
Adversus Marcionem. Trans. P. Holmes. Edinburgh: T & T Clark, 1868.
Adversus Praxean. Trans. E. Evans. London: SPCK, 1948.
Apologeticus. Trans. T. R. Glover. London: Heinemann, 1931.
The Apostolic Fathers. Trans. J. B. Lightfoot and J.R. Harmer. Michael Holmes, ed. Grand Rapids: Baker, 1989.
Biblia Sacra Iuxta Vulgatem. R. Weber, ed. Stuttgart: 1975.
De Anima. J. H. Waszink, ed. Amsterdam: Meulenhoff, 1947.
De Carne Christi. Trans. E. Evans. London: SPCK, 1956.
The Divine Institutes. Trans. Mary Francis McDonald. Washington: Catholic University of America Press, 1964.
De Resurrectione Carnis Liber. Trans. E. Evans. London: SPCK, 1960.

II. SECONDARY SOURCE MATERIALS

Altaner, B. *Patrology.* Trans. Hilda C. Graef. Edinburgh-London: Nelson, 1960.
Arnold, E. V. *Roman Stoicism: Being Lectures on the History of the Stoic Philosophy with Special Reference to Its Development within the Roman Empire.* Cambridge: Cambridge University Press, 1911.
Ayers, Robert H. Language, Logic and Reason in the Church Fathers: A Study of Tertullian, Augustine and Aquinas (*Altertumswissenschaftliche Texte und Studien* Series: No 6). Georg Olms Verlag, 1979.
Aune, D. *Prophecy in Early Christianity and the Ancient Mediterranean World.* Grand Rapids: Eerdmans, 1983.
Bardenhewer, O. *Patrology: The Lives and Works of the Fathers of the Church.* Trans. Thomas J. Shahan. St. Louis: B. Herder, 1908.

Barclay, J. M. G. *Jews in the Mediterranean Diaspora: From Alexander to Trajan (323 BCE-117 CE)*. Edinburgh: T & T Clark, 1996.
Barker, M. *The Great Angel: A Study of Israel's Second God*. London: SPCK, 1992.
Barnes, T. D. *Tertullian: A Historical and Literary Study*. Oxford: Clarendon Press, 1985.
Barrett, C. K. *Essays on John*. London: SPCK, 1982.
Bediako, K. *Theology and Identity: The Impact of Culture upon Christian Thought in the Second Century and in Modern Africa*. Oxford: Regnum Books, 1992.
Berkhof, L. *Systematic Theology*. London: Banner of Truth, 1971.
Bernard, L. W. *Justin Martyr*. Cambridge: Cambridge University Press, 1967.
Bethune-Baker, J. F. *Introduction to the Early History of Christian Doctrine*. London: Methuen, 1919.
Bettenson, H. *Documents of the Christian Church*. London: Oxford University Press, 1963.
Braun, R., ed. *Chronica Tertullianea et Cyprianea, 1975-1994: Bibliographie critique de la première littérature latine chrétienne*. Paris: Institut d'études augustiniennes, 1999.
Bray, G. *Holiness and the Will of God: Perspectives on the Theology of Tertullian*. Atlanta: John Knox Press, 1979.
Brown, H. O. J. *Heresies: Heresy and Orthodoxy in the History of the Church*. Peabody: Hendrickson, 1998
Burgess, S. M. *The Holy Spirit: Ancient Christian Traditions*. Peabody: Hendrickson, 1984.
Campenhausen, H. V. *The Fathers of the Church*. 1 vol. Peabody: Hendrickson, 1998.
Carrell, P. R. *Jesus and the Angels: Angelology and Christology of the Apocalypse of John*. Cambridge: Cambridge University Press, 1997.
Carrington, P. *Christian Apologetics of the Second Century*. London: SPCK, 1921.
Chadwick, H. *The Early Church*. London: Penguin, 1993.
Colish, M. L., *The Stoic Tradition from Antiquity to the Early Middle Ages*. 2 vol. Leiden: Brill, 1985.
Cross, F. L. *The Early Christian Fathers*. London: Gerald Duckworth, 1960.
Copleston F. *A History of Philosophy: Greece and Rome*. Garden City: Image Books, 1962.
Daniélou, J. *A History of Early Church Doctrine before the Council of Nicaea*. 3 vol. London: Darton, Longman & Todd, 1964–77.
Dooyeweerd, H. *A New Critique of Theoretical Thought*. 4 vol. Amsterdam: Paris, 1953-58.
Dunn, J. D. G., *Christology in the Making: A New Testament Inquiry into the Origins of the Doctrine of the Incarnation*. London: SCM Press, 1980.
────── *Jews and Christians: The Parting of the Ways*. Grand Rapids and Tübingen: Eerdmans and J.C.B. Mohr (Paul Siebeck), 1999.
Ehrman, B. D. *The Orthodox Corruption of Scripture: The Effect of Early Christological Controversies on the Text of the NT*. New York and Oxford: Oxford University Press, 1993.
Evans, C. S. *The Historical Christ and the Jesus of Faith: The Incarnational Narrative as History*. Oxford: Clarendon Press, 1996.

Farrar F. W. *Lives of the Fathers: Sketches of Church History in Biography.* 2 vol. Edinburgh: A&C Black, 1889.
Ferguson, Everett, ed. *Doctrines of God and Christ in the Early Church*: Studies in Early Christianity. vol. 9. New York: Garland Publishing, 1993.
Floyd, W. E. G. *Clement of Alexandria's Treatment of the Problem of Evil.* London: Oxford University Press, 1971.
Fortman, E. J. The Triune God: A Historical Study of the Doctrine of the *Trinity.* Grand Rapids: Baker, 1982. Reprint. Eugene: Wipf and Stock, 1999.
Fox, M. V. *Proverbs 1–9: A New Translation with Introduction and Commentary.* New York: Doubleday, 2000.
Frend, W. H. C. *The Rise of Christianity.* Philadelphia: Fortress Press, 1984.
———·*The Donatist Church: A Movement of Protest in Roman North Africa.* Oxford: Clarendon Press, 1952.
Gieschen, C. A. *Angelomorphic Christology: Antecedents and Early Evidence.* London: Brill, 1998.
Gonzalez, J. L. *A History of Christian Thought.* 3 vol. Nashville: Abingdon, 1970.
Goodspeed, E. J. *A History of Early Christian Literature.* Chicago: University of Chicago Press, 1942.
Grant, R. M. *The Early Christian Doctrine of God.* Charlottesville: University Press of Virginia, 1966.
———· *Gnosticism and Christianity.* New York: Harper and Row, 1966.
———· *Gods and the One God: Christian Theology in the Greco-Roman World.* London: SPCK, 1986.
Grillmeier, A. *Christ in Christian Tradition.* Trans. J.S. Bowden. London: A. R. Mowbray and Co., 1965.
Gundry, R. "Angelomorphic Christology in the Book of Revelation." SBL Seminar Papers 33 [1994] 662–678.
Hall, S. G. *Doctrine and Practice in the Early Church.* Grand Rapids: Eerdmans, 1991.
Hale, William G. and Carl D. Buck. *A Latin Grammar.* Tuscaloosa and London: University of Alabama Press, 1903.
Hannah, D. D. *Michael and Christ: Michael Traditions and Angel Christology in Early Christianity.* Tubingen: Mohr Siebeck, 1999.
Hanson, R. P. C. *The Search for the Christian Doctrine of God: The Arian Controversy, 318–381 AD.* Edinburgh: T & T Clark, 1988.
Harnack, Adolf. *History of Dogma.* 7 vol. London: Williams & Norgate, 1894–1899.
Hatch, Edwin. *The Influence of Greek Ideas and Usages upon the Christian Church.* London: Williams and Norgate, 1898.
Hazlett, Ian, ed. *Early Christianity: Origins and Evolution to Ad 600.* London, 1991.
Heine, R.E. *The Montanist Oracles and Testimonia.* Patristic Monograph Series 14. Macon: Mercer University Press, 1989.
Hengel, M. *The Son of God: The Origin of Christology and the History of Jewish-Hellenistic Religion.* London: SCM Press, 1976.
———. *Judaism and Hellenism: Studies in their Encounter in Palestine during the Early Hellenistic Period.* 2 vol. London: SCM, 1974.

Hurtado, L. W. *One God, One Lord. Early Christian Devotion and Ancient Jewish Monotheism*. Philadelphia: Fortress Press, 1988.

Johnson, P. *A History of Christianity*. London: Weidenfeld and Nicolson, 1976.

Jonas H. *The Gnostic Religion: The Message of the Alien God and the Beginnings of Christianity*. Boston: Bacon Press, 1963.

Jones, H. C. *History of Christian Doctrine*. Edinburgh: T & T Clark, 1978.

Kearsley, R. *Tertullian's Theology of Divine Power*. Carlisle (Edinburgh): Paternoster (Rutherford House), 1998.

Kelly, J. N. D. *Early Christian Doctrines*. Edinburgh: Adam and Charles Black, 1958.

Knight, J. *Disciples of the Beloved One: The Christology, Social Setting and Theological Context of the Ascension of Isaiah*. Sheffield: Sheffield Academic Press, 1996.

Lacugna, C. M. *God for Us: The Trinity and Christian Life*. New York: HarperCollins, 1991.

Lincoln, A. *Ephesians*. WBC. Waco: Word, 1990.

Lintott, A. *Imperium Romanum: Politics and Administration*. London: Routledge, 1993.

Little, S. *The Christology of the Apologists*. London: Duckworth, 1934.

Lonergan, B. *The Way to Nicea*: The *Dialectical Development of Trinitarian Theology*, Trans. Conn O'Donovan. London: Dartman, Longman, and Todd, 1976.

Longenecker, R. N. *The Christology of Early Jewish Christianity*. London: SCM Press, 1970.

MacMullen, R. *Christianizing the Roman Empire* (A.D. 100–400). New Haven and London: Yale University Press, 1984.

Margerie B. *The Christian Trinity in History*. Still River: St. Bede, 1982.

Melick, R. *Philippians, Colossians, Philemon: An Exegetical and Theological Exposition of Holy Scripture*. NAC. Nashville: Broadman Press, 1991.

Mellone S. H. *Leaders of Early Christian Thought*. London: Lindsey Press, 1954.

Metzger, B. M. *The Canon of the New Testament*. Oxford: Clarendon Press, 1997.

Milman H. H. *History of Latin Christianity: Including that of the Popes to the Pontificate of Nicolas V*. 8 vol. New York: W. J. Widdleton, 1870.

Moltmann, J. *Trinity and the Kingdom*. Trans. Margaret Kohl. London: SCM Press, 1981.

Morgan, J. *The Importance of Tertullian in the Development of Christian Dogma*. London: Kegan Paul, Trench, and Trubner, 1928.

Murray, G. *Five Stages of Greek Religion*. Garden City: Doubleday, 1955.

Newman, J. H. *An Essay on the Development of Christian Doctrine*. London: Blanchard and Sons, 1846.

Noll, S. F. *Angelology in the Qumran Texts*. University of Manchester: Ph.D. Diss., 1979.

O'Collins, G. *Christology: A Biblical, Historical, and Systematic Study of Jesus Christ*. Oxford: Oxford University Press, 1995.

———. *The Tripersonal God*. Mahwah: Paulist Press, 1999.

Olson, R. *The Story of Christian Theology: Twenty Centuries of Tradition and Reform*. Downers Grove: InterVarsity Press, 1999.

Olyan, S. *A Thousand Thousands Served Him: Exegesis and the Naming of Angels in Ancient* Judaism. *Tübingen: J.C.B. Mohr (Paul Siebeck)*, 1993.
Osborn E. *Tertullian, First Great Theologian of the West*. New York: University Press, 1997.
Pagels, E. *Gnostic Gospels*. London: Weidenfeld and Nicolson, 1979.
Pelikan, J. *The Christian Tradition: A History of the Development of Doctrine*. 5 vol. Chicago: University of Chicago Press, 1971–1989.
———. *The Shape of Death: Life, Death, and Immortality in the Early Fathers*. London: Macmillan, 1962.
Poirier, John C. "Montanist Pepuza-Jerusalem and the Dwelling Place of Wisdom." *Journal of Early Christian Studies* 7 (1999) 491–507.
Pokorny, P. *Colossians: A Commentary*. Peabody: Hendrickson, 1991.
Prestige, G. L. *God in Patristic Thought*. London: SPCK, 1952.
Quasten, J. *Patrology*. 3 vols. Utrecht: Spectrum, 1962–64.
Reumann, J. "Martin Werner and 'Angel Christology'." TLQ 8 (1956), 349–358.
Richardson, C. C. *The Doctrine of the Trinity*. New York: Abingdon Press, 1958.
———. *The Christianity of Ignatius of Antioch*. New York: AMS Press, 1967.
Roukema, R. *Gnosis and Faith in Early Christianity*. London: SCM Press, 1999.
Rives, J. B. *Religion and Authority in Roman Carthage from Augustus to Constantine*. Oxford: Clarendon Press, 1995.
Roberts, R. E. *The Theology of Tertullian*. London: Epworth, 1924.
Rowe, N. J. *Origen's Doctrine of Subordination: A Study in Origen's Christology*. Peter Lang, Berne, 1987.
Rudolph, K. *Gnosis: The Nature and History of an Ancient Religion*. Trans. Robert M. Wilson. Edinburgh: T & T Clark, 1983.
Sadowski, F, ed. *The Church Fathers on the Bible: Selected Readings*. New York: Alba House, 1987.
Salisbury, Joyce E. *Perpetua's Passion: The Death and Memory of a Young Roman Woman*. New York: Routledge, 1998.
Sanders, J. *The God Who Risks: A Theology of Providence*. Downers Grove: InterVarsity Press, 1998.
Schoedel, W. R. *Ignatius of Antioch: A Commentary on the Letters of Ignatius of Antioch*. Philadelphia: Fortress Press, 1985.
Seeberg, R. *Textbook of the History of Doctrines*. Trans. Charles E. Hay. Grand Rapids: Baker Book House, 1966.
Sider, R. *Ancient Rhetoric and the Art of Tertullian*. London: Oxford University Press, 1971.
Stead, G. C. *Divine Substance*. Oxford: Clarendon Press, 1977.
———. "Divine Substance in Tertullian." *JTS* N. S. 14 (1963) 46–66.
Stuckenbruck, L. *Angel Veneration and Christology: A Study in Early Judaism and the Christology of the Apocalypse of John*. Wissenschaftliche Untersuchungen zum Neuen Testament. Martin Hengel and Otfried Hofius, ed, vol. 70. Tubingen: JCB Mohr (Paul Siebeck) 1995.
Studer, B. *Trinity and Incarnation*. Trans. Andrew Louth. Edinburgh: T & T Clark, 1993.

Tabbernee, W. *Montanist Inscriptions and Testimonia: Epigraphic Sources Illustrating the History of Montanism*. Macon: Mercer University Press, 1997.

Talbert, C. H. "The Myth of the Descending-Ascending Redeemer in Mediterranean Antiquity." *NTS* 22 (1976), 418–440.

Tillich, Paul. *A History of Christian Thought*. Trans. Carl Braaten. London: SCM Press, 1968.

Tixeront, J. *History of Dogmas*. 3 vol. St. Louis: B. Herder, 1910–1916.

Trakatellis, D. C. *The Pre-Existence of Christ in Justin Martyr: An Exegetical Study with reference to the Humiliation and Exaltation Christology*. Missola: Scholars Press, 1976.

Trevett, C. *Montanism: Gender, Authority, and the New Prophecy*. Cambridge: Cambride University Press, 1996.

Vos, H. F. *Exploring Church History*. Nashville: Thomas Nelson, 1994.

Walker, Williston. *A History of the Christian Church*. New York: Charles Scribner's Sons, 1970.

Warfield, B. B. *Studies in Tertullian and Augustine*. New York: Oxford University Press, 1930.

Warner, R. *The Greek Philosophers*. New York: Signet, 1958.

Werner, M. *The Formation of Christian Dogma*. London. Adam and Charles Black, 1957.

Wiles, M. *The Making of Christian Doctrine: A Study in the Principles of Early Doctrinal Development*. London: Cambridge University Press, 1967.

———. *Archetypal Heresy: Arianism through the Centuries*. Oxford: Clarendon Press, 1996.

Wilken, R. *The Myth of Christian Beginnings*. London: SCM Press, 1979.

Williams, D. H. "The Origins of the Montanist Movement: A Sociological Analysis." *Religion* 19 (1989) 331–351.

Wolfson, H. A. *The Philosophy of the Church Fathers*. Cambridge: Harvard University Press, 1956.

Wright, N. T. *The New Testament and the People of God*. Minneapolis: Fortress Press, 1992.

Wypustek, A. "Magic, Montanism, Perpetua, and the Severan Persecution." *Vigiliae Christianae* 51.3 (1997) 276–297.

III. LEXICA AND GENERAL AIDS

Dictionnaire Latin-Français Des Auteurs Chrétiens: Revu Specialement Pour le Vocabulaire Théologique. A. Blaise. Brepolis: de Strasbourg 1954 [1993]).

A Greek-English Lexicon of the New Testament and other Early Christian Literature Revised and edited by F.W. Danker. Chicago: University of Chicago Press, 2000.

A Latin Dictionary. Founded on Andrews' Edition of Freund's Latin Dictionary. Revised, enlarged, and in great part rewritten by Charlton T. Lewis, Ph.D. and. Charles Short, LL.D. Oxford. Clarendon Press. 1879.

A Patristic Greek Lexicon. G.W.H. Lampe, ed. Oxford: Clarendon Press, 1961–1968.

Index

angelic christology, 1
angelomorphic christology, 1
angelophanic christology, 2

Carthage, 87
Clement of Alexandria, 28–29
consors, 89

derivatio, 65
Die Enstehung des Dogmas, 2
Docetism, 24–25

Ebionites, 32–34
ex officio, 8

fiat lux, 58, 80

Gnosticism, 19–20

Hippolytus, 24

in tempo, 81

Jewish angelology, 4

malak YHWH, 6, 79
Milman, Henry, 82
minoration, 30

modalistic monarchianism, 43
monarchy, 10–12
Montanists, 45–46

natality angels, 4

Patripassianism, 44, 47
Perpetua, 5
persona, 83–84
portio, 73–74
Praxeas, 41–42

ratio, 53–54, 57–58
rule of faith, 23, 43, 87–88

sermo, 54–55
Sophia, 55, 85
Stoicism, 81
substance, 65–67, 84–87

Tatian, 26–27

ut natura, 9

Valentinus, 20–23

Werner, Martin 2–3

Biographical Sketch of Author

Edgar Foster received his B.A. from Lenoir-Rhyne College in Classical Languages and Philosophy. He earned a M.Th. from the University of Glasgow in Scotland and is currently writing a Ph.D. dissertation entitled *Naming, Metaphor and Paternitas: The Concept of Divine Paternity in the Thought of Lactantius*. He has also authored Christology and the Trinity.

www.ingramcontent.com/pod-product-compliance
Lightning Source LLC
Chambersburg PA
CBHW020658300426
44112CB00007B/428